THE WILD CURE

FROM DEATH TO LIFE ON OREGON'S LONGEST RIVER

Dean Hall

with Bre Hall

foreword by Thomas P. Seager, PhD

Beach Cottage Publishing, LLC

Copyright © 2023 by Dean Hall and Bre Hall

All rights reserved.

No portion of this book may be reproduced in any form without written permission from the publisher or author, except as permitted by U.S. copyright law.

This publication is designed to provide accurate and authoritative information in regard to the subject matter covered. It is sold with the understanding that neither the author nor the publisher is engaged in rendering legal, investment, accounting or other professional services. While the publisher and author have used their best efforts in preparing this book, they make no representations or warranties with respect to the accuracy or completeness of the contents of this book and specifically disclaim any implied warranties of merchantability or fitness for a particular purpose. No warranty may be created or extended by sales representatives or written sales materials. The advice and strategies contained herein may not be suitable for your situation. You should consult with a professional when appropriate. Neither the publisher nor the author shall be liable for any loss of profit or any other commercial damages, including but not limited to special, incidental, consequential, personal, or other damages.

Cover Photos: Stephen Cridland

Other Photos: Stephen Cridland and Steven Tyler

ISBN (paperback): 978-1-960626-00-4

ISBN (e-book): 978-1-960626-01-1

For Mary

FOREWORD

The story you are about to read is unpossible, which is a new word I am borrowing from an old episode of *The Simpsons* to describe something that is so far removed from expectation that there is no way a person could have contemplated ahead of time a world in which this story could exist.

Most medical doctors will tell you not to believe it, definitely do not attempt it, and even just the retelling of it could be dangerous to your health and sanity.

That's probably why Dean Hall considers it a miracle.

The problem is that I don't believe in miracles.

I'm a man of science. I spent over six years in engineering graduate school, training my brain in the scientific method so that I could arrive at rational, repeatable explanations for how the physical world works. I earned my Doctor of Philosophy in Civil Engineering over 20 years ago and since then I've published over 150 articles in scientific publications.

When I first heard Dean's story of curing his cancer after swimming the entire length of the Willamette River in Oregon, I thought, *he must be exaggerating*.

Dean seemed like a sincere guy, and I was sure that *he* believed his story, but that didn't mean I was signing on to it like he was some kind of modern medical miracle.

And I still don't.

Because, as I found out and will discuss with Dean later on in the book, his seemingly miraculous experience has a reasonable scientific explanation.

I first met Dean in 2018, when he discovered the ice bath company I co-founded, called Morozko Forge. At that time, there was no such thing as an ice bath that could make its own ice, and my partners and I wanted one, so we invented it.

Dean must've been doing his homework, because he discovered our email address and sent us a note asking if we would consider a promotional partnership. Not knowing anything about marketing affiliates, or coupon codes, or social media, we said, "what the heck," and built Dean a Forge. He was our first customer to whom we couldn't deliver ourselves, and it seemed at the time like he knew more about deliberate cold exposure than we did, so we figured maybe we'd learn something.

But there was also something more personal to it for me.

Dean's story resonated with me because I had just been through a prostate cancer scare. A little over a year earlier, as part of a routine blood panel, I'd had my prostate specific antigen (PSA) tested, and the results frightened me. They were elevated enough to suggest that I should be getting a prostate biopsy.

I decided to talk to other men before I talked to a doctor. I was afraid that as soon as I made contact with the allopathic medical establishment, they might put me on a one-way trajectory into overdiagnosis, excessive intervention, and risky, uncomfortable surgery.

I wanted to know what I was getting into, before I set in motion a chain of medical events that might be difficult to undo.

To my surprise, almost every man I spoke with had a prostate story, including some younger than me at the time (early 50s) who'd had prostatectomy. Their stories were not encouraging.

Long story short, I resolved to exhaust every non-surgical intervention I could find before I would agree to so much as a biopsy, and to monitor my PSA levels to gauge the results of my self-experiments. Instead of consulting a doctor, I increased the frequency of my deliberate cold exposure, extended my fasts, and reduced my carbohydrate intake, so I could cycle myself in and out of keto. And it worked.

By the time I met Dean, my PSA dropped to levels so low I was no longer considered at risk, and as a happy coincidence, my testosterone levels shot through the roof. But I considered myself lucky, not clever. After all, the PSA test is notoriously unreliable, and just because I'd had one elevated result didn't mean I ever had cancer. So I reasoned that my improvement was probably an illusion—the result of a testing anomaly—rather than a reliable prescription that could serve as an example to others.

Getting to know Dean changed my mind on that.

He inspired me to go back to the library and understand the metabolic mechanisms and origins of cancer for myself, and to document both our stories as a way to encourage others to share more of their experiences, too.

You might not know that Dean is a licensed marriage and family therapist, who specializes in guiding people to resolution of trauma, but if you ever have the chance to meet him, you'll sense the compassion and empathy in him right away. He is the type of person who inspires you to believe that there is a power hidden deep inside you upon which you, too, can draw, no matter what sort of logjam has been thrown in your path.

The true miracle in Dean's story is not in his cure, remarkable as it is. For me, if there is a miracle, it is in the relationships that form between people that have an energetic connection that transcends the world of science. It is in the unmeasurable quality of life that brings people together for reasons that may never become obvious, even after the fact, but nonetheless present us with an opportunity to change the course of our lives for the better.

In this book, you're going to read about Dean's harrowing escapes from the dangers of the river. You're going to read about the support from his friends and family that enabled him to keep swimming, and some of the moments when they thought they may have lost him.

You're going to read about the grief he felt whenever he was reminded of his first wife's death from cancer. You're going to read about a man who felt he had nothing to lose and wanted to do little more than inspire other terminal cancer patients to live every last moment they had left to the fullest.

What you're not going to read is that Dean was monitoring his lymph nodes, or drawing his blood for testing, or concerning himself in the least with his diagnosis. He didn't have time for that during his swim.

What was happening in Dean's spirit may have been a miracle, but what was happening in his body is subject to scientific description I will discuss with Dean later on.

For now, it is my hope that, in reading his book, you experience just a fraction of the inspirational energetic connection I have felt with Dean over the years.

Thomas P. Seager, PhD
Co-founder, Morozko Forge
Associate Professor, Arizona State University

AUTHORS' NOTES

Dean Hall

> "There are only two ways to live your life. One is as though nothing is a miracle. The other is as though everything is a miracle."
> —Albert Einstein

This quote by Einstein has become one of my favorites. In fact, I've dedicated years of my life to finding miracles in every little thing and inspiring others to do the same. So, it's hard to imagine the first time I discovered this quote I spent several long minutes cussing out Einstein for being totally wrong.

Why was I doing something so uncharacteristic and outlandish as cussing out a German theoretical physicist I had never, and would never, meet?

To say I was at a low point in my life is an understatement.

Three years before my discovery of Einstein's quote, I had lost the first, and most important, of many treasures in my life: my wife of nearly thirty years. What quickly followed was the loss of my community, my private therapy practice, and, finally, my health. I had long given up viewing anything, much less everything, as a miracle. So, the day I found his quote, I thought it was the stupidest thing I'd ever heard, and I let Einstein have it with both barrels, calling him every name in the book.

What's changed my mind since then? How did I go from hating this quote to trying to live by its example?

The first-hand accounts in this book will answer those very questions. You will see, not only through my eyes, but the eyes of those closest to me on my journey, exactly how I went from viewing nothing as a miracle, to viewing everything as a miracle.

It is my hope that the stories in this book will inspire you. Maybe you feel like you've lost everything. Or perhaps you're facing a difficult diagnosis of your own, or that of a loved one. Or possibly you simply need to see someone else dive all in on a dream in order to dive all in on your own. Wherever you're at in your journey, wherever you're coming from today, I believe there is something in this book that will speak directly to you.

This story is my own, but it is not unique to me. I am convinced, like me, you have everything you need to wake up, dive in, and realize you, too, are swimming in miracles.

Bre Hall

Since I have two degrees in creative writing and write novels for a living, my dad had been asking me for years to write about his historic swim on the Willamette River, and for years I had been putting him off. I told him to write it himself. That it wasn't my story to tell. And he tried to put the story down into words, but he never seemed happy with anything he came up with.

The project sat idle for over a year.

Then, the night before I was meant to fly to London and visit a friend, COVID-19 shut down the world. I was staying the night at Dad's house so he could drive me to the airport the next morning, and, instead of catching a flight, I suddenly found myself in lockdown with him and my stepmom, Bobbi. Like almost everyone else, we expected lockdown to last for a week, maybe two. And when I couldn't return to work, weeks in isolation became months. During that time, I finished the draft of one of my novels faster than I'd anticipated and quickly found myself without a writing project.

If you spend only a few minutes at my dad and stepmom's house you will notice at least one element that nods to Dad's history with long-distance swimming or his love for water in general. Dad's own abstract waterscape paintings adorn the walls. Photographs of a wetsuit-clad man popping his head out of a river are hidden here and there. Then there's the Morozko Forge ice bath in the garage. The damp swim towel and wetsuit jammers hung over the stair railing. The nose plugs and goggles and bottles of swimmer's ear rolling around at random in the back seat of Dad's car.

During lockdown, everywhere I turned there was another reminder of the stuff my father was made of. The grit and determination and vision and water—yes, I'm fairly certain Dean Hall is made of river water by now—and I started to ask myself, *why not?* Why not write Dad's story down? He'd given me so many things throughout my childhood and young adult years, why not give him the gift of story?

I'd heard the tale of the summer he attempted to become the first person to swim the entire length of the Willamette River in Oregon with two active forms of cancer so many times I thought it would be easy to write down. I borrowed the journal he had kept from that time. I scoured social media for the daily posts he'd made during his swim. I eavesdropped from the next room as he shared his story with several podcasters.

I sat down and wrote start after start after start, changing perspectives and voices and angles so many times it was ridiculous. After months, I decided nothing was working. None of it felt right. There was something missing. But what?

One day it clicked. The missing element was simple: genuine, first-hand accounts of Dad's swim. Not just from Dad, either, but from those closely involved. His parents, his sister, friends and strangers who helped him along the way, me.

What follows is an oral history of my dad's 2014 Willamette swim. The majority of the interviews I conducted were done one-on-one, either in-person, over the phone, or via video chat between the summers of 2020 and 2022. A handful of interviews were done in small groups—I don't think my grandparents would have let me interview them separately for fear of the other missing out on reliving those good times.

So many years had passed since the time I conducted the interviews and the swim that some of the people who had been involved didn't feel their memory of that time was strong enough to be of much use or, simply, we couldn't track them down, so a few key voices are missing, and for that I am sorry, not just to you, the reader, but to the story and its integrity.

Time is a funny creature, isn't she? She has the capacity to erase our memory as well as distort it. Keeping that in mind, there are portions of the book where there is conflicting information regarding certain events. Grandpa remembers it one way, Dad another. Honestly, those are some of my favorite parts, because it highlights the fact that we all remember our lives differently and that there is not just one truth in this world, but many.

It should be noted that I have edited all of the interviews for the sake of brevity and clarity. The spirit of this story and its message, however, have remained intact.

PART I

"Can you see the beauty of being alive?

Will you find the courage to catch my current?

Are you ready to dive in and swim away with me?"

~Mama River Whispers

ONE

Dean Hall (*swimmer, cancer survivor*): What does it mean to truly be alive?

I think that's what most of us wonder as we go through our daily routines. What does it mean to be alive? Why don't I feel alive most of the time? When I do feel alive, why don't I enjoy life? For me, the answers to those questions are tied to nature, to water, to rivers.

Rivers are alive. They're constantly moving forward. They're not resisting or fighting anything. Rivers move around, over, and through. When a river is blocked, it waits with quiet patience, slowly building until it slips over and continues its journey.

There is a dreamlike quality to plunging into wild waterways. Flashes of color scattering and refracting. Icy fingers rolling over and past you. Like a siren's song, living water calls out to the water trapped inside you, tempting it to remember the freedom of easy movement, encouraging you to find your flow. Like a loving mama, water whispers the way back to life. This I know firsthand.

In 2013, I'd become so sick with leukemia and gotten so boxed in by the poor decisions I'd made after the loss of my wife three years earlier that my life had become stagnant. I wasn't moving like a river. I didn't feel alive.

I was born four blocks away from the Willamette River in Portland, Oregon. The deep, wide shoulders of that blue-green current were always a part of my consciousness growing up. Ever since I was a little kid I would swim across lakes and rivers, imagining someday swimming something even larger and longer.

When anyone jumps on a big dream there are usually precursors—little glimpses into who they are and what they're going to do. We all come to this earth with a destiny, and the compass that points to that destiny is our hopes and dreams.

Still, in the thousands of times I had crossed over the Willamette River or driven along it, I had never imagined the wild journey I would someday take in its waters.

Bre Hall (*Dean's daughter*)**:** I believe everything happens at just the right time in life.

That was Dad and the Willamette. It happened at the perfect time. A time when he had been completely stripped down, tested to his core, and needed a way to return to himself, a way to rebuild.

Dean: In August of 2013 I was dying of cancer. I was getting thinner and thinner and losing more and more weight. My lymph nodes had swelled way up. The lymph node itself didn't really hurt, but the ones under my jawline and the one under my right armpit had ballooned to such a size that it made it difficult to move.

One day, I was in the bathroom, and I made the mistake of looking in the mirror. When I did, I hardly recognized the man staring back. He had dark circles under his eyes, huge swollen jowls under his jawline where the lymph nodes had puffed up so much that his face almost went straight down into his shoulders—he hardly had any kind of neck. Then, I looked into his eyes, and he just looked so sad.

At that point, I was done. I thought, *you know if I let the leukemia take me no one would ever know that I gave up. I could just let nature take its course.*

I was almost resigned to that idea. Then, I looked myself in the eyes again and thought, *no you've got a twenty-one-year-old daughter who just lost her mom to brain cancer a few years ago. It would be entirely selfish to continue this line of reasoning. She deserves better.*

Death was a luxury I couldn't afford. I had to keep living. I had to be a good father. I could not leave my daughter alone. So, I decided to do whatever I could to live.

I knew having a purpose you were passionate about had the power to bring you back to life. So, I started praying and almost begging God for a purpose. To me, it made sense to write a book because I'd written one. It made sense to build a new therapy practice because I'd done that before. It made sense to do all sorts of things, but I couldn't get passionate about any of them. I knew, unless it was something that gripped me, something that could make my heart leap, that it wouldn't hold any power over me.

For weeks, several times a day, I would stop in prayer and ask God for a purpose. For something, anything, and it was just…silence.

Finally, I found an old notebook I had been forced to keep in the sixth grade. At the very first I had written: *when I become an adult, I just gotta*—it didn't even say want to or have to, it was gotta—*climb Mt. Everest and swim the English Channel.*

I had forgotten how passionate I was as a child about becoming an adventurer as an adult. I wanted to be someone who swam channels and climbed mountains. I just assumed, until I was in my mid to late teens, that adventuring was what my career would be. However, life quickly became all about hard work and responsibility and, because of that, I abandoned what I had felt were childish dreams of adventure.

But when I found that old journal I started thinking about adventuring again.

I knew I didn't have the money or the strength to climb Everest. I figured it would take ten or fifteen thousand dollars, and, being an active cancer patient, the high altitude would be nearly impossible for me. But, for some reason, swimming the English Channel seemed totally reasonable.

Of course, I tried to come up with every reason not to do it. I tried to prove how silly of an idea it was. But every time I would think about it my heart would jump—it literally would leap—and I thought, *okay, this is what I've got to do.*

I called up my GP, Dr. Watters, and told him what I was planning.

"Dean," he said, "You get in a public pool, with your immune system worn down from the leukemia and it will kill you."

I sort of yelled into the phone, "What do you want me to do, then? Die on the couch watching *Wheel of Fortune*? I'm not going to do that."

He said, "Well, you know, I don't know what to tell you then, but you're going to have to be very careful, and I don't know how you can be careful in a public pool, so take what I say into consideration."

Dr. Aaron Watters, M.D. *(Dean's general practitioner)*: Dean was critically ill when he first started thinking about swimming. His mental and physical health were both pretty bad, actually, and his diet was poor. So we had several long discussions about him getting into the pool.

Dean: A few days after I talked to Dr. Watters, I decided to get into the pool anyway. What did I have to lose? Really?

I went over to Cascade Athletic Club in Gresham, close to where my parents lived in Portland, in late August and had my first swim.

At that time, I was thinking about swimming the English Channel. The Channel was about twenty miles long, depending on how you hit the current and everything. That first day I knew I couldn't swim twenty laps, but I could swim twenty lengths. One length for every mile in the Channel. Ten laps total. I promised myself I'd get in and swim those laps no matter how long it took me.

I jumped into the pool and immediately spit into my goggles, which was what a lot of old-school swimmers did because, back in the day, we didn't have defogging spray. I just dropped a little spit into each lens and rubbed it around with my thumb. There was something about just being in the water and going through an old ritual that made me feel good. Then, I turned around and kicked off the wall.

Bre: I don't think Dad told anyone what he was doing at first. Not really. Which is odd because he loves to share his dreams with everyone. Looking back, I think he just wanted to make sure it was even possible.

I often wonder what his life, and even my life, would look like if he had never gotten into that pool.

Dean: Kicking off of the wall, putting my hands in front of me, gliding out into the lane—it was such a deeply engrained muscle memory from all the hundreds of miles I'd swum in my life. It made me feel alive for the first time since my wife, Mary, died.

That first lap was glorious.

I felt my body moving. I felt a little bit of power.

Then, I got to the other side, went to kick off, and—nothing *[laughs]*. All of my power was gone, but I had to make it to the other side. I just had to. My strokes were slow, but eventually, I finished that first lap. Then, I stopped and stood there with my arms flopped onto the pool deck just gasping for air. It probably looked creepy, but there was a giant smile on my face, because, even though I was breathing hard, I felt alive.

Once I caught my breath, I kicked off the wall again and felt great for about half the length before my energy left again. I struggled to get to the other side. I stopped at that end of the pool and thought, *okay, I'll just do this one length at a time, but damn it, I'm going to get to twenty.*

Nowadays, ten laps takes me about ten minutes, but that first time it took me an hour. It was ridiculous. And, in typical

Hall fashion, when I got to my last lap and was kind of congratulating myself, I heard my dad say, *is that all you got, really?* I thought, *okay, if I'm really going to do this I gotta stretch myself.*

I had nothing left in the tank, but I did one more lap.

I walked out of that pool a changed man. I felt strong, like I was slipping back into my identity, like I was recovering a part of me I thought had been lost.

Richard Hall (*Dean's father*): He didn't share with me that he was lost somewhere out in the wilderness.

Alice Hall (*Dean's mother*): No, he didn't say much about it.

Richard: He didn't share that he needed an anchor. But I knew swimming had always been an interest and he always had a bent for the unusual. He'd always been an adventurous guy. Conquer the world and all that stuff.

As a kid, Dean was the one who had all of the imagination and creativity and artistic abilities—he could do anything.

Alice: He was the one who did most of the talking in the family, that was for sure.

Dean: When I was a little kid, we'd be backpacking and we'd come across an alpine lake. Mom and Dad would always say, "Dean, I bet you can't swim across that lake."

I think the first time we did that I was nine or ten maybe.

I'd always jump in and swim all the way across. Every now and then, I'd look up to see if Mom was looking, you know, the way kids do. When I'd get out, they'd cheer and congratulate me and warm me up.

I always thought they encouraged me to swim the lake because they liked to see their children challenged. I thought they were training me to do something great in the future. But it was just two years ago I realized that wasn't it at all. I just hadn't shut up on the trail for five hours and they wanted a little time to themselves, a little quiet. They knew if I was face down in the water, they'd get ten or twenty minutes without having to hear me talk.

Richard: Dean was always on some edge of mischief. Anything that was exciting or challenging.

Lisa Tyler (*Dean's sister*): I've always felt that Dean was a big dreamer.

He makes his dreams sound so easy and simple and doable. As his sister, I never want him to get hurt or be disappointed, and I remember, at first, thinking how big of a dream his swim was, and how I couldn't imagine him doing that, especially with him being so sick. I mean, how do you persevere through something like that? In my mind it's crazy, and in Dean's mind it's an adventure.

Bre: For the longest time it was all about the English Channel. Then, one day, it all shifted.

Dean: As I was training to swim the Channel and thinking about logistics, it became apparent how difficult it would be to go over to England, fundraise—I always wanted to raise money for a cancer foundation—in a foreign land, find a team over there, and then get it swum.

It just didn't feel right.

So, for two weeks, I prayed, "How can I do this but do it in a way that makes a bigger impact?"

One day I was getting out of the pool, and the thought occurred to me, *who cares if another middle-aged man puts on a speedo and swims to France? It does the world no good, and, in my case, it's not even a pretty picture.*

Sure, it would have been fun to go halfway across the world and swim the English Channel, but it wouldn't have felt quite so organic.

Within a day or two after thinking and praying about that, an ancient dream came back. As soon as I thought about it, I couldn't believe that it hadn't been my first choice.

In 1984, I was living in Kansas but came back to Portland for the summer. I remember we were having a family picnic in West Linn and Dad and I were standing up on a hill, looking out over the Willamette River. At the time I was twenty-four and deeply into my triathlon mode, thinking about swimming, biking, and running all the time. I said to Dad, "Has anybody ever swum this whole thing?"

He looked up at me and said, "That is the stupidest idea I've ever heard. Where do you come up with this crap?"

He berated me just enough to really sink the hooks deep, and I thought, *okay, now I've gotta do it.* Without even knowing it, he was throwing the gauntlet down.

Richard: No, I don't remember that, but I wouldn't put it past him to have asked such a thing.

Alice: Dean remembers things that we don't, but I think that same summer he'd gone swimming in the Willamette, and I think he mentioned that he'd like to swim the whole river someday.

Dean: After that day in West Linn, I started poring over maps of the Willamette, reading as much as I could on it. Then, I went back to Kansas and started my first year of teaching in Dodge City, but in my spare time I was still looking at maps of the river and thinking and talking to my wife, Mary, about the next summer, or the summer after, going back to Oregon and swimming the whole Willamette.

Finally, I think Mary had had enough of me obsessing about it. She said, "Dean, how long will this take?"

"I don't know," I said. "Twenty, twenty-five days probably."

"How will you pay for it?"

"I don't know."

"We need money right now and, even though you're a teacher, you have to work in the summer because you don't make enough during the school year. We need to save up money for a house, not for you to swim a river."

I thought about it and realized she was probably right.

I wish now I would have said, "No, the house can wait," or, "It's not going to cost that much." Which, it wouldn't have, especially back then.

But I might not have been ready, and the river might not have been ready, so I put that dream aside and focused on my life in Kansas.

Bre: Growing up, I often wondered how a guy like my dad ended up in Kansas at all. It was the complete opposite of the Pacific Northwest.

Richard: After high school, Dean moved to Kansas to play soccer. He was a really good soccer player. Could have gone anywhere.

Dean: I chose Kansas of all places to play soccer because it was far from home and I loved history. Kansas seemed to have a lot of interesting history, with the land rush and even the Civil War, so I thought it would be fun to get another picture of American history as it applied to Kansas. Plus, I thought it might be my *Green Acres* experience, you know.

I went there thinking I'd be there for a year or two, not knowing I would meet this cute little Kansas girl at college and fall in love.

When I asked Mary to be my wife, she firmly told me, "I love you, but I'm not just blindly moving up to Oregon because that's where you come from. I'm very close to my family. I'm not moving away from them. You know, I didn't go up to Oregon, you came down to Kansas. I love you, but if we're going to get married, I need you to know that I'm not going up there."

So, I went back to Portland for a summer and thought about what she had said. I came to the conclusion that, as beautiful as Oregon was, with its mountains and rivers and trees, and as much as I loved it, it didn't seem like anything without Mary.

Dad talked to me long and hard about it. He said, "I know you love her, but I don't think you understand what you're getting into."

I went back to Kansas in August 1980 and married her in November. But Dad was right—I had no idea what I was assigning myself to. Basically, I was putting myself in exile for love. *[Laughs]*.

If Oregon was my version of heaven, Kansas was my version of hell.

Even before I met Mary, when I first landed there from Portland, I'd never seen anything so flat. To me, there were no rivers no lakes no hills no trees. To be fair, there were some trees and some tiny hills, but not like back home. It felt like I'd been dropped on the face of the moon, especially where my college was in western Kansas. Out there it's just flat. Nothing but dust and endless wheat fields.

When I talked to people who were from Kansas, they'd say when they went to Colorado or Oregon or a place that was heavily forested they'd feel very claustrophobic, but, for me, being in such a wide-open space made *me* feel claustrophobic. The whole time I was out in Kansas, all thirty years, I felt that way. I learned to live with it, but I was just out in the middle of nowhere, in a desolate landscape, and it made it hard to breathe. It felt like there was no life, and what little life that was there, like the trees—they were stunted compared to the eighty to one-hundred-foot-tall Douglas Firs I'd grown up with. So, to me, all life was struggling to scrape by in Kansas, myself included.

One of the reasons I married Mary was because she seemed to fulfill my biggest dream in life, which was to recreate what I saw my parents have and that was a relationship where they really loved each other and loved going on adventures together. When I met Mary she was funny, winsome, quick. She was unlike any other woman I'd ever met before in my life. She had a funny way of saying things. She'd make many words up and use them in interesting ways.

Bre: Because of her twangy accent, milk was a two syllable word to my mom. *Mi-ilk*. Or she'd use the German word for milk her grandma had taught her: *milch*.

She'd say, "they talked my leg off," instead of, "they talked my ear off."

When I'd eat too much sugar she'd say, "Oh, Breanne, you're gonna glow in the dark."

Dean: Mary was an extremely hard worker, and I respected that about her. She had a never say die, never give up mentality that very much fit into the "Hall" ethic.

When we got married we were young. I was barely twenty.

Once I finished college, I started teaching, but, being a teacher, it meant we were still very, very poor and constantly struggling, but even though we were struggling, we would have told you we were very happy.

Within our first year of marriage, we made a list of twelve things we had to do or see together. I think we ended up only doing two of the twelve things over the thirty years of our marriage. It didn't completely surprise me. We were always putting fun things off to do the hard work of building wealth, planning for retirement, being responsible. We both got our degrees and started teaching. Then, I decided to go back to school and get my degree in Marriage and Family Therapy. I'd teach full-time during the day, then I'd go to work at night building a private practice in the local community. For thirty years that's what we did. We paid our dues.

Then, just as it seemed like all of those dues were finally going to turn into gold and we were gonna get to enjoy the fruits of our labor, Mary was diagnosed with an inoperable brain tumor and died two weeks before our thirtieth wedding anniversary.

Bre: When I was young I used to tell people my mom was my best friend, and they'd just laugh at me.

But it was true.

My mom was always on the move, and I think anyone who knew her would tell you she moved *fast*. After school, I was either outside with Mom doing yard work or in the passenger's seat of her car running errands around town. If it was a weekend, Dad was usually with us, but during the week, when he was always working, it was just Mom and me.

I told Mom everything that was going on in my life, even if that meant getting in trouble for something I'd done. We'd laugh, we'd cry, we'd yell at each other, we'd forgive each other easily, we'd invent our own inside jokes.

My mom was the funniest, kindest, most-loving, most-giving person I've ever known. I learned a lot about how to treat people from her. She didn't care who the other person was or what background they came from or if they were decked out in diamonds or literally covered in chicken shit; she'd talk to them as if none of that mattered. Half of our errands involved taking meals to families going through difficult times or giving rides to those without cars or visiting elderly shut-ins from our church.

My mom was the bright spot in so many people's lives, but she was my sun. She was the thing my life revolved around for so long. And when she was gone, just like that, I felt like my entire world had collapsed in on itself.

I was seventeen when Mom died. After she was gone, everyone kept telling me how strong I was, but I knew I wasn't. I was lost. I was numb. I no longer felt alive.

I know Dad felt the same way, too.

Lisa: It was really hard after Mary died *[pauses, voice cracks]*. As Dean's sister, *[starts to cry]* just to see the love of his life go, and being back in Oregon and so far away, it was really hard, because I just wanted him to be okay.

Richard: When Mary passed away, Alice and I were there and we saw, but it's one of those things that, even though we were close, we were still on the outside of that emotional shell and not inside that shell where Dean and Bre were.

Dean: It happened so fast, and she had been so healthy it never occurred to me that she might be the one to get sick and die. We always talked about what it would be like when *I* died, especially since I'd had leukemia before. We never expected it to be her.

I was really lost for a while after that.

I made a series of horrible decisions, and I believe some of those decisions adversely affected my health.

By the time I was thinking about swimming the Willamette in 2014, I was more than ready for something positive to focus on in my life.

Dr. Watters: Dean and I were both at the lowest points in our lives during that time. He was still battling the death of Mary.

I remember we met up and talked about this vision quest that he had. We agreed it was about getting his body and soul in the right place to allow him to heal.

The more time he spent in the pool training, he started to seem so much better physically and mentally.

Dean: I was finally ready to put everything I had into focusing solely on this dream that was meant to bring me back to health and back to life. I was ready to start training seriously for the Willamette. I was finally ready for the journey I was destined to take.

*"Move with me,
flow into life, and
let go of gray—
become blue."*

~Mama River Whispers

TWO

Dean: Imagine a beautiful blue highway with every shade of blue and green you can think of. That's what I think of when I think of the Willamette. It's a very wild river and, at the same time, a comforting, serene river.

Richard: There's history along the Willamette, with pioneers and Native Americans and fur traders. Everybody congregated around it, and it sort of became the beating heart of the state.

Alice: First of all, it is not pronounced *will-a-met*. It's *will-am-it*. I don't think most people outside of Oregon realize that.

It runs south to north and I don't think there are too many rivers like that, not in the United States anyway.

In Independence, Oregon, where I grew up, our family farm was right beside the Willamette. We always called it our river. Of course, we never went swimming in it. When I was a kid it was too dirty to do that sort of thing.

Travis Williams (*executive director of Willamette Riverkeeper*): The Willamette River Basin is a system that has been simplified, so all those side channels that used to be there naturally, that would rise with spring floods and fall in the summer, are gone. They still have a connection hydrologically to the river, but a lot of those have been cut off over time, and that's effected the river's ability to provide habitat.

Dean: In very few places does it have whitewater, so, for most of its course, it just silently moves along. Calmly. Quietly. A nurturing mother, a caretaker.

Bre: I'm a Kansas girl, so, before we moved to Oregon, the rivers I'd known were dark and murky and full of filth, but the Willamette River is the complete opposite. It's just this gorgeous emerald gem twisting through the state.

Travis: Even though it's a river in the most populous valley in the state of Oregon, you could be out there at times and you might hear an airplane in the distance or maybe a piece of farm equipment but you could kind of feel like you're distant from this busy place.

Lisa: Before Dean's swim, to me, the Willamette was the river where all the bridges were as you crossed into Portland, but because of my brother the river has forever changed in my mind.

Dean: I thought swimming the Willamette would be the perfect tribute, if you will, to the Pacific Northwest and the state of Oregon. It would be a way to honor the immense beauty this part of the country has to offer. Plus, it had never been swum in its entirety. The historian in me liked the idea of being the first person in history to do something.

But you don't just swim a river. You don't just slip into the current one day and start heading toward the Columbia. No. You have to put in the long hours. You have to take the steps that edge you closer to that final test. So, I spent hours in the pool training and hours at home praying and meditating.

I started out small. Eleven laps became eighteen became twenty-one. Slowly, I was upping my distance. Slowly, I was picking up the pace.

Dr. Watters: The type of cancer Dean had was CLL, Chronic Lymphocytic Leukemia. Sometimes people do well with that and sometimes people do poorly. When Dean started training he was at the peak of doing poorly with all that stress, poor diet, lack of exercise, but then I started to see a change in him.

When he said he wanted to swim the entire Willamette I knew it didn't have the cleanest water and would be a difficult number of miles, so I was a little concerned. But how are you going to tell somebody, when they're getting better from the therapy they're doing that they shouldn't do it, you know?

Any challenge that you put in front of Dean he's going to conquer.

Dean: Very soon, training became a matter of willpower. There were so many times my brain would scream, *why are you doing this?* At that point, everybody, even family, was asking me that question. Nobody really was supporting my dream. I knew I had the stubbornness and the grit to pull it off, but those early training days were difficult, especially once I started picking up speed. You'd think the more you picked up speed the better you'd feel about what you were doing, but I still had that voice in my head, doubting.

On March 3rd of 2014 I turned fifty-four, so I decided to swim my age, which now doesn't seem like a big deal, but at the time it seemed gigantic, because I knew I'd probably be swimming right at an hour. Usually at that point my swim stroke would fall apart. I was still getting used to total immersion swimming, where you don't kick as much, so I'd average right at a minute a lap, which wasn't very fast. I knew if I was going to swim my age, it would take over an hour of constant swimming. But I promised myself I wouldn't stop until I got to fifty-four.

The Willamette was almost 200 miles long, but on my birthday I thought, *man I'm swimming a long ways, swimming a mile and a half. [Laughs]*. Fifty-four laps sounded like 500 to me.

I remember getting to the locker room and changing into my swimsuit and being so nervous. Nobody knew. I hadn't told anyone. But I was nervous because I knew if I struggled and wasn't able to swim that far my idea of swimming the Willamette that summer was just ridiculous and couldn't happen.

But I did it, and it felt like a grand celebration. The best present I could have given myself for that birthday.

Right after I broke that barrier, I very quickly started swimming two miles, which is seventy-two laps, and that seemed crazy to me. I was swimming about an hour and fifteen minutes at a time continuously, and it seemed to take forever. Then, I jumped it up to three miles, which is 108 laps, and that was probably the hardest part of my training. Any time I'd touch the wall after finishing a lap I'd think, *lap one down, 107 to go.* It would get so boring and took so much time. It just felt like I would never be done.

I found that so much of ultra-endurance work is really mental. The reason I can do what I do is mostly because I've learned, when your body is tired and making excuses, you just don't have a conversation with that part of your mind.

During the time I was training for the Willamette, I would meditate once a day for about an hour, and I would visualize myself swimming into the Columbia River and being super happy. I would see myself being able to swim the whole river. I would see myself getting strong. I would see myself getting up every day and not whining and complaining but being happy and looking forward to each day on the river.

Even with the meditation, training was still difficult. It was just pounding out mile after mile after mile in the pool. I started hearing that voice in my head saying, *hey you can take the day off. It's no big deal. Why don't you just watch movies tomorrow and not go swimming?*

My mantra became: The extraordinary becomes possible when you make it impossible to remain ordinary.

Since I didn't have a TV in the house and used my computer to watch movies, I would pack my swim bag the night before, take it and my laptop out to my car, and put the bag on top of the computer. That way, if I listened to the voice in my head and wanted to watch movies, I'd have to confront the swim bag first. Usually, I'd just get in the car and drive to the pool anyway.

I had also started a blog on Facebook and was up to about 500 followers. I'd post how many laps I was going to do the night before and then follow up with how many I actually completed. That, combined with calling my dad and telling him the same information, kept me accountable.

Richard: It was a mixed bag of thoughts when Dean was talking about swimming the entire length of the Willamette. I thought, *well maybe he's thinking from Salem or Oregon City onward*, but when he went back to the source in Eugene, I thought, *he's bitten off more than he can chew.*

I really thought he was out of his mind.

He's always thought big, all growing up. Always had these wild ideas. I just thought this was another dream he wanted to do, but I really didn't know if it was possible because of his cancer; but, knowing Dean, I also didn't discount him either.

Dean: In February, when I shifted my dream from the English Channel to the Willamette, the first people I ended up telling was the charity I decided to fundraise for.

I wasn't the only one in the family who had leukemia. Since the early 2000s my dad had been living with cancer as well. What's really odd is that Dad and I ended up with the exact same type of leukemia. Every oncologist I'd ever seen told me that type of leukemia is not genetic and that it's very rare to see two people in a family have Chronic Lymphocytic Leukemia, especially a father-son duo. But we both had it. That's why, when I was searching for charities, the Leukemia and Lymphoma Society felt like the natural fit.

What really made me choose them, though, was I emailed the director of the Portland chapter and told her that I was swimming the entire Willamette and wanted to raise money for LLS. Within two or three hours I had an answer from her. She had invited me to come in and talk about my plans.

Here's a guy who has leukemia and lymphoma, is in his fifties, doesn't have any swim records under his belt, and who no one knows. Then I say I'm going to swim the entire length of the Willamette River and, not only is this director welcoming, but, once she finds out I'm not crazy, she is all about trying to make this work. She got really excited about it and was super supportive.

LLS sat down with me two or three different times to talk it over. I was planning on swimming it in July, but their biggest fundraiser of the year, The Man/Woman of the Year, happens in May and June. I immediately said no because I didn't want to be anyone's man of the year—I didn't want it to be about me.

"Well, Dean," they said. "It's really not about that. You can direct attention away from yourself if you want to, but the only reason we're suggesting you participate is that it's a huge campaign and a lot of other people will be raising money around the same time. Then, we have a gala event at the end of June and find out which person and their team has raised the most money in that six-week time frame. Whoever has is honored by being named the man or woman of the year."

So, I agreed and started to put together a team.

Richard: Dean sort of tiptoed into the conversation about the Willamette with Alice and me. He said, "I'm going to swim the river, and I'd like to raise money for the Leukemia and Lymphoma Society. They have a meeting that's coming up, and I'd like you to go with me."

I thought, *well, I'll go and listen to it and at least see what it's all about.*

It was an organizational meeting for everybody that was going to participate in raising money for LLS that year. Everyone else's plan was to go off and drum up money from friends and companies. Then the conversation got to Dean. He told them he was going to swim the river. He was going to have an active part in this fundraising. It was so different from everyone else that I thought, *oh Dean-o, what in the world did you get yourself into*—and I thought *your*self, meaning just him, but all of the sudden it became *our*-self. He wanted Alice and I involved as well. *[Laughs].* I just couldn't believe it.

Dean: I knew I needed a safety boater, someone in a kayak, to guide me down the river. Someone who would be a good leader. Someone I could trust with my life.

I immediately thought of my dad. He had spent his whole life adventuring. He knew how to make critical decisions out in the wilderness, where you have no one else to rely on but each other.

A guide boater is a leader and a guide but also a personal assistant in a way. Someone who knows when it's time to stop, rest, and refuel. Being a marathon runner and mountain climber Dad knew the thin line between pushing your limits and going too far. I knew he'd know when it was time to get out and stop and warm up. That's critical. If you go too far you might not be able to swim the next day or your body might break down in the next week. You have to walk that fine line between endurance and insanity.

But Dad didn't immediately say yes.

In fact, in early March, Dad and Mom were trying to decide whether to go all in or all out. I think they were trying their best to get me to call off the swim, but, in typical fashion, they were praying about it and asking God to give them wisdom. They were praying along the lines of: *if somebody joins Dean on this thing then we'll see that as a clear sign that this is what Dean is supposed to be doing and we'll jump in and help however we can.*

Around that same time the director of the Leukemia and Lymphoma Society recommended I get in touch with Willamette Riverkeeper.

Travis: Willamette Riverkeeper is a nonprofit organization founded in 1996. The general idea is to protect and restore the Willamette River's water quality and habitat.

Dean: I had tried to contact them before, but hadn't had any luck. The director of LLS said she knew the people who worked there and said they were wonderful. She encouraged me to drop in on them sight unseen and, if anything else, they would make an appointment for me to come back.

So, I decided not to wait, but I hate cold calling anyone. It comes back from my old cub scout days where we'd have to go door to door asking for donations or selling mistletoe. I almost talked myself out of dropping in on them, but I knew they'd have vital information I'd need about the river. I thought to myself, *if you're going to do this thing, you've got to just take the plunge.*

I walked into their office unannounced. The first person I met was Kate. She'd been an Alaskan river guide and had also kayaked the Colorado—I mean, she was accomplished. It was fun to meet her because she was that interesting combination that you see many times only in adventurers, where they're really quiet and maybe even soft spoken but underneath they're just steel. I talked to Kate for a little while, and she was really interested in what I was going to do. Initially, she told me the director, Travis, was busy. Their office is a series of cubicles, and the one in the farthest corner belonged to Travis, and, without me knowing it, he had been listening to what Kate and I were talking about. All of a sudden, this swarthy, strong, athletic guy—the kind of guy you can imagine deep in the woods or out on a river, a man's man—comes out of his cubicle with this wide grin on his face.

Travis: When Kate and I met with Dean the first time, we talked over the potential issues in terms of safety. Depending on the time of year, how would he be able to stay warm enough? How would a swimmer deal with a fast current when it's going into a large piece of wood or a tree or that kind of thing? Those questions are ones we think about a lot when we're talking to people about canoeing or kayaking or stand-up paddleboarding. The same exact stuff applies to a swimmer. To me, I was wondering if that would work for Dean. Just being able to look ahead is what it's all about.

Dean: He ended up giving me about an hour to an hour and a half of his time. He gave me maps and a book he'd written about the Willamette. He said he could help find me river guides for the dangerous portions up near Eugene. He was so excited.

Then we got into some nitty-gritty details. He said, "Run through with me where you plan to start and end."

"I plan to start up in Eugene, at the source," I said.

"The first three miles are fairly dangerous," Travis said. "Lots of rapids and shallow, rocky sections."

At the time, I imagined dozens of swimmers swimming the entire Willamette after me. I didn't want to encourage anyone to go through a section of the river that could pose a threat to their life. So, I decided to take Travis' advice and shave off the first three miles.

"Where do you plan to end your swim?" he asked next.

"That's what I wanted to talk to you about," I said. "I'm thinking about stopping at the Hawthorne Bridge."

"What? Why would you do that?" he asked.

The area from the Hawthorne Bridge in Portland to Sauvie's Island had once been one of the worst hazardous waste sites in America. The river had been poorly managed for many decades, really from Portland's infancy in the late 1800s, but especially for most of the 1900s, when sewage and industrial waste was dumped into the river unregulated.

However, in the 80s and 90s the federal government set up a superfund site to clean up that dangerously toxic area.

"I'm worried," I told Travis, "that, with my leukemia, swimming through that area will cause irreversible damage to my immune system."

Travis sort of shook his head at me. "Dean, that's in the sediment, and they've done a lot to even clean that up. But you're going to be moving with the current at the top of the river. Now, if you were twenty feet down maybe it would be a hazard, but unless there's a blue algae bloom, or sewage overflow, or something like that, you're going to be in very clean water. Just as clean as it is up in Eugene. You don't want to stop at the Hawthorne Bridge only to have some other guy swim the river a month after you and say that you didn't do it all."

Travis: You could still go get a water sample from the Newberg area and find dozens upon dozens of toxic compounds at de minimis levels. They're not going to be harmful to you or me, but if you think about fish basically breathing and filtering that water every day or someone who's in the water a lot over time, it just proves there continues to be a case to do better for the Willamette. Dean's swim proved that in a way, too.

Dean: It was Travis who talked me into swimming into the Columbia River, and, it was his support that prompted Dad and Mom to get involved as well. Travis was their sign that they should be a part of my swim.

Richard: I still thought it was a crazy idea, but after he told everyone at the cancer meeting about his plans, had gotten the support of Willamette Riverkeeper, and wanted me involved, I thought, *you can either be a discourager or an encourager and Dean has already been through enough*, so I decided why not be an encourager and see how far we go? If we get just past Eugene at least we've done something.

After that, we started to put the pieces of the puzzle together. We knew full-well Dean was going to concentrate on swimming and I would sort out all the logistics.

Alice: Richard studied maps of the river. Figured out each day. You know, where would be a feasible in and out.

Richard: Was there a boat ramp we could use? Was there a dock? What kinds of food and drink would Dean need to keep going for an entire day of swimming?

Alice: Richard also made phone calls to hotels for reservations and to see if they'd let us have any money off since Dean was swimming for charity.

Richard: As we started to piece this thing together we realized this ordeal wasn't just a couple of days. We were talking an entire month. That meant there'd be a lot of driving and a lot of buying of food.

Alice and I were getting up there in years and, even still, Dean hooked us into something that was way over our heads.

Alice: And I was just a year out from that horrendous experience I'd had with osteoporosis and my back, so I wasn't very well off physically.

Richard: The swim came at a time when we were—

Alice: Seventy-nine.

Richard: We look back now and think, man—

Alice: How did we do that?

Richard: How did we do it, and boy, was that at the right time in our lives or what? That both of us still had the energy and tenacity to keep it up day after day.

Alice: *[Laughs]*. Yeah.

Richard: It was a thrill. One of our greatest—

Alice: Highlights.

Dean: Once Dad and Mom jumped on board the momentum of this thing really got rolling. I dropped off the maps Travis had given me with Dad and asked if he would divide the river up into sections. Mom wanted to be involved, too, so, at first we decided she would be one of the organizers of the fundraising portion of my swim, but later she became our driver.

Lisa: When Dad got involved in the swim, Dean got excited.

You know, Dean and I are so far apart in age that I don't know if we experienced all the same kinds of things growing up, but I think I can speak for both of us when I say that when Dad was all in on something we were doing, we felt invincible. Like we could do anything, big or small.

Dean: It's funny. The bigger the dream you have and the more impossible it seems, the less people you have who want to support you at first. Not only that, but everyone tries to talk you out of it. Nobody is encouraging. You feel totally alone. You constantly wonder if it's worth it, and it's agonizing.

But then, if you refuse to quit, it's like life hands you little gifts for not giving up.

I got to meet Travis, and that was a huge gift. Dad and Mom went all-in to support me, and that was a gift. But the biggest gift was that I just wanted to have something to concentrate on other than my loss of Mary, the stupid decisions I made afterward, and my fears of dying and leaving Bre all alone. All I had wanted was some place positive for my mind to focus, and what had started out as small and personal suddenly became so much bigger than I could have even imagined.

Everything was falling into place, but I still hadn't tested out the river. No matter how monotonous and difficult training in the pool was, no matter how hard finding others to support my dream had been, the river was more challenging than I could have imagined.

One of my favorite quotes is by Yvon Chouinard: "It's not an adventure until something goes wrong."

Boy, that was true about the Willamette from the beginning.

*"There is no need to fight.
There is always a way
around, past, over, through.
Let your heart be guided by water."*

~Mama River Whispers

THREE

Dean: Dad had never kayaked. I had never swum a river. We definitely hadn't done it together. We knew we needed to get into the Willamette and practice finding our rhythm.

Richard: A spot that was familiar to us was Independence.

Dean: Mom had grown up there. We also thought it would be fun because my cousin Jon lived in Salem and could join us in his canoe. It wasn't an extremely turbulent or difficult passage of water, and it was only about three miles from the boat launch in Independence to the place we would stop for the day, so we thought it would be a good first run.

It was a gray, drizzly April day. We'd had a lot of rain, so the water was moving fast.

Richard: I was there with the kayak and Jon showed up with the canoe. We were sort of paddling around the dock waiting for Dean when I thought, *man, this river has a stronger current than I thought it did.*

Dean: At the time, I was trying to hold onto the idea of creating a world record in the eyes of the world's open water swimming associations. They would not officially count any swim that used any kind of assistance, especially wetsuits, because they give extra buoyancy and that is considered a cheat.

Richard: Dean stripped down to just his swimming suit, and then he was ready to go, you know. *[Laughs]*. But it wasn't exactly a warm spring day.

Dean started to get into the river. A foot went down, then another. Up to the ankle.

He looked at me and said, "Boy, this is colder than I thought it would be."

Dean: The way I remember it, Dad and Jon left me with the boats so they could take Dad's truck down to the place we would end up, that way we'd have a shuttle back to the boat launch. As I was waiting on them to get back I decided to get into the water.

I got in mid-torso and thought, *I can't stand here for long.*

I was freezing.

So, I backed up to where the water was just about to my knees and stood there.

About ten minutes later, Dad and Jon came back and got in their boats. By that time, though, I couldn't feel my feet. It made it hard walking down the boat ramp. As a matter of fact, I only took four or five steps and did a real shallow dive—I wasn't even at the end of the boat launch—just because I couldn't feel my feet enough to walk any further.

Richard: Dean got into the water a little deeper and said, "Man, this is really cold, Dad."

"Well, so what?" I said. "It's cold. That's what you've got ahead of you."

"Okay," he said, then plunged into the river and started swimming.

Dean: As soon as I put my face into the water, I thought, *uh-oh, I might have bitten off more than I can chew.* Then I thought, *No, it's all about mental toughness. Focus. Don't panic.*

But it was so cold it was hard not to panic.

I started swimming.

About fifteen minutes into it that thing I started having hypothermic aspirations, and I'd never experienced that before. It was frightening. My whole body convulsed and I halfway threw up. All of the air was expelled from my body.

I took my head out of the water and did the breaststroke. Within a couple of seconds, I'd start to warm up, but then I'd put my face down in the water and *[snaps fingers]* immediately it would feel like brain freeze. Within a few strokes I'd have hypothermic aspirations again.

I went through that routine five or six more times.

I knew the signs of deep hypothermia. I couldn't feel my face. I couldn't really feel my arms or legs. I was starting to shiver. Dad started talking to me and I was having a hard time making sense of what he was saying. I could hardly answer since my lips were numb.

Richard: Dean reached a point when he finally knew he was in over his head.

He said, "Dad, I've got to get out of the water, because I am getting chilled right to the bone. It's not a good thing."

Dean: It was so embarrassing. My cousin Jon had to pretty much drag me over the side of his canoe and paddle me back to the boat launch. He was laughing at me and calling me Papa Smurf because I guess I was actually blue.

Richard: I was trying to paddle the kayak back to shore, struggling. Jon was really having problems in the canoe. Dean was shivering and blue. I thought, *this could be the three stooges out here.*

Jonathan Clark (*Dean's cousin*): I remember them asking me to take my canoe, but I don't remember much about that day. It's like looking into the fog of the past. *[Laughs]*.

Richard: Eventually, all three of us got back to the boat launch. Dean was just *brr*, shivering so bad.

Dean: We decided to try and save the day somehow by going out to lunch in Salem. The whole time I was trying to make pleasant conversation, but I just wanted to scream, "I blew it. I'm screwed. I don't know what I'm doing."

Finally, the quiet desperation welled up within me, and I quickly went to the bathroom. I just burst into tears in the bathroom stall, thinking, *I've lost my whole life. I've lost everything. This was my one great hope, and I think it's absolutely impossible—what am I going to do?*

I couldn't come up with anything that seemed like a reasonable solution to the cold, other than I could die trying. But, by then, the whole reason I was doing the swim was to inspire other people to go after their dreams, no matter the circumstance, and to console my daughter. To let Bre know I was coming back to life. To die trying went against that bigger plan, but I didn't feel like I had any other options.

So, I went back to the table and was able to kind of fake it through the rest of lunch.

Later, when I got into Dad's truck I was still shivering. He turned the heat up on high. He even had an extra vest, a blanket, and a beanie. I put all of those on to try and warm up.

On the way home, I acted like I was dozing because I didn't want to talk. I was literally sitting there with my eyes closed, screaming at myself. I was in such a frustrated, miserable state about how the practice run had gone.

Twenty minutes away from home we got stopped in traffic on the freeway. I opened my eyes and Dad asked, "How are you doing?"

"Not good," I said.

"Are you still cold?"

"Yeah, I'm a little cold, but that's not the problem."

"Well, what's going on?" Dad asked.

Richard: On the way home, Dean said, "This changes the whole complexion of the swim, because I can't swim in that kind of water—in that cold stuff—day after day and survive. That cold would just take it out of me."

Dean: I said, "Dad, I failed. This is the first practice swim and I couldn't even make it to the first bend in the river. I don't know what I'm going to do."

I expected him to scream back at me or tell me to buck up and be a man, but he just was quiet for a little while. I thought, *oh here it comes.*

But Dad just quietly and very matter-of-factly, like it was no big deal, said, "You'll get a wetsuit."

It was quiet for a while. Then, all of my stress just poured away.

I almost laughed at how simple that answer was, how logical.

The very next Monday, we went to talk to Travis at Willamette Riverkeeper. He asked, "How did your practice swim go?"

We told him, and he laughed.

I said, "Yeah, I don't see any way I can do this without a wetsuit."

"Oh, I've thought that all along," he said.

"Yeah, but Travis," I said. "It's not going to be a world record if I use a wetsuit."

He just stopped, looked at me, furrowed his brow, then said, "That's not what you're about anyway, Dean, is it? Is that why you're doing this? Do you really need to have your feat confirmed by some little old men sitting in an ivory palace in London or someplace? Is that what you've got to do? I didn't think you were that guy."

I looked at Dad, then I looked at Travis. I said, "You're right, I'm not."

"Then wear a damn wetsuit," Travis said.

Travis: It's one thing to have someone roll their eyes or think, *geez, why is this person doing this?* It's another thing to be supportive, so at Willamette Riverkeeper, we were encouraging.

Dr. Watters: I really didn't think Dean would swim the whole river. The odds were stacked against him. If I remember right, the weather was rough, the water was colder than he expected.

But he was just not going to give up.

Dean: I picked up a wetsuit from Athlete's Lounge in Portland the week after the first practice swim. They didn't charge me anything. Just let me borrow it for the swim.

Man, I loved that wetsuit. I had put on a wetsuit a time or two in the 1980s and, one time, even tried to take a few swim strokes, but it was nearly impossible. But the suit Athlete's Lounge donated for the swim was made specifically for swimming, for triathlons. It made me feel superhuman.

That weekend, Dad and I went back down to Independence for another trial run, this time with the wetsuit. It was still rainy and cold. The river was moving fast, but not as fast as it had been the time before. Just as I started swimming, the sun broke through the clouds.

As soon as I put my face down in the water, particularly with the neoprene cap on my head, the water felt so warm and so good. I felt the way I did when I was a kid and had a new pair of P.F. Flyers—I felt like I could run faster and jump higher.

I made it around the first bend in no time. I was just flying, or at least it felt that way.

For the first time, I really felt the power of the river. It was moving me around quite a bit. I hit some whirlpools and swells in the current. That was strange, because I'd be swimming along and then I'd hit a swell and the river would push my whole body up toward the surface and then, after a few strokes, it would drop me back down to where I'd been. I had never felt that before. It was a little unsettling at first, but I thought, *you better get used to this because you've got almost two hundred miles of it.*

Even during that first swim I started to embrace the feeling of the water being alive and having its own life and personality. When I'd swum in lakes or pools or even oceans I'd never had the feeling of symbiosis, where I was being guided by the water, like I was in the Willamette. It was like a beautiful dance. It was easy to get into this perfect state of flow. Being face-down in the crisp, wild water, watching a kaleidoscope of colors beneath the surface and hundreds of massive Douglas fir trees spinning by on shore, was like nothing I'd ever experienced before.

Richard: We finally got to the place where we were stopping for that trial run. It wasn't even a boat ramp. Just the side of the river where a lot of fisherman were.

Dean: They weren't casting or anything, but they had lines in the water and were standing on this steep ten, fifteen-foot cliff of mud. The river was going fast and those fishermen were right where we needed to be to get out.

Richard: I said to Dean, "I'm not going to mess with any of the fishermen, but I'm going to go right where I want to go in."

Dean: Dad started paddling through all these fishing lines.

Richard: Boy, they were not too happy, but I came in there with the kayak and sort of beached it just a little bit before Dean got out of the water.

There were a couple of guys that were very aggressive. One of them said, "What in the hell are you guys doing?"

Dean: As I was swimming up to where I was going to climb out of the river, I heard some guy yelling profanity at Dad. I thought, *uh-oh we're in trouble, because Richard Hall is not just going to quietly put up with this.*

Dad didn't say much, but then the guy came back again and started giving him the mouth. I heard Dad calling him pal, which is Dad's way of saying the fight's on.

Richard: I told this guy, "My son has cancer, he is going to swim the Willamette River in a couple of months, and this is one of his trial swims."

"Well, we're fishing here," this guy said.

"I don't care what you're doing, pal," I said. "I'm kayaking and my son is swimming. Do you have a problem with that? Do we have to take it further? We screwed up a couple of lines—so what?"

Dean: Dad isn't a big guy—5'7", 5'8"— but he's the most intimidating person I know. He especially was when he was younger. Sure, he was ripped, but it was also his demeanor. I never saw him actually get in a fight, though, because everybody would back down pretty quickly, because they were scared of him.

One time, I was a junior in high school and playing on three different soccer teams. I'd been doing a lot of weightlifting and had pretty good-sized biceps and shoulders, a big chest. I was in the best shape of my life. I thought I was tough, a real scrapper. I thought I could take the old man.

So, Dad's sitting at the table on a Saturday morning, reading the paper and I started shadowboxing all around him.

"Stop that," he said quietly.

I tapped him on the head.

"What did you just do?" he asked.

I tapped him on the head again.

"Don't ever do that again," he said.

Of course, I went to do it a third time—I didn't see him move. All of the sudden I was on my back, his knee was on my chest, and he had his thumb on one side of my Adam's Apple and his fingers on the other side, choking me out.

Nose to nose with me, he said, "I told you not to do it again. Are you ever going to do that again?"

I could barely choke out, "No."

So, when that fisherman was getting mad at Dad, I thought, *oh boy, here we go*. I was tired, I'd just had this wonderful experience in the river, and I didn't want to mar it with a bunch of conflict, so I didn't jump into the conversation immediately. I got out of the river, went over to Dad's truck, and started stripping off my wetsuit.

Richard: Pretty soon, Dean came whipping up there out of the water. He's sort of impressive, how big he is, then there was me, a little short guy ready to dupe these guys out. Dean said, "Dad, we got a problem?"

"I don't think so," I said, then looked at those guys. "Do we have a problem?"

Dean: I look over and there are about five guys standing around Dad and he's in the center of them. I thought, *okay looks like we're going to have some conflict here. I better go over.*

Having swum five miles, I'm all pumped up, and I thought, *okay, it's on. Looks like we're going to scrap.*

My wetsuit is stripped down to my waist, so I tied my sleeves around my back and tucked them in so nobody could grab 'em. I go over there, almost peacocking. I've got my shoulders back, my pecks out. I've got "The Hall" stare-down face on. I'm ready to go.

Then I hear Dad say, "Oh, here he is." Dad said something else and all of these fishermen laughed like they were having a party.

I thought, *how did it turn from conflict to everybody having a great time that fast?* They were laughing and talking to Dad, then I introduced myself and one of them said, "Man, keep in touch. This has been great."

This has been great? You're the guy who was calling my dad names.

That's Dad, too, though. You think you're about to scrap, then suddenly you become best friends.

I couldn't help but think how fitting it was that our first real practice swim almost ended in a brawl. It just fit. The rest of the trial runs didn't get much easier, but they had less conflict, that was for sure.

The next practice swim I did was from Clackamette Park, down by Oregon City, to Willamette Park, close to Portland City Center. It was nine miles total, our longest trial swim. There was about a mile to go—I could see the park—and I pooped out. I didn't make it. I just had nothing.

There was a steep embankment nearby with access to a road. Dad said, "I'll go ahead and go to the boat launch and get the car and bring it to this road."

"I'll walk up and meet you there," I said.

After Dad paddled off, I started to feel really bad. I thought, *I can't even make it nine miles and we're planning on going twelve to fifteen a day?* But when I told Dad that, he said, "Hey, it's still early in the process. We're getting used to this. You might need to pace yourself more, but you're going to get stronger. It's no big deal."

We decided not to tell anyone—this is the first time I've ever admitted that I didn't make that one.

Travis: Dean had the motivation, he was doing the research, and Richard was right there with him, along for the ride. Then there were some safety boaters that came out of the woodwork. Some good folks, like Al and Lou, who jumped in.

Al Grapel (*swiftwater rescuer*)**:** Travis called me to see if I wanted to be involved.

Louis English (*swiftwater rescuer*)**:** Then Al recruited me after Travis had talked to him.

Al: I pulled Lou in…or down, I guess. *[Laughs]*.

Dean: I think Travis wanted to make sure my swim was a success, and the first part of any success is not dying. He wanted to make sure we were being safe. He was mostly concerned with the first section of river from Eugene to Corvallis, because it's more of a wild river in those early miles. So, he set us up with Al and Lou, who had been paddling the Willamette for years and were both kayaking legends in the Eugene area.

Al: I'm a landscape architect. I went to forestry school for that and started working for the forestry service. It was then I realized there were a lot of places I wouldn't get to see unless I was on a river.

Louis: I started kayaking in 1972.

I bought a sea kayak—no one had a sea kayak in Eugene back then—and then I took a white water class through the Eugene Parks so I could learn to roll my kayak.

Really, the most kayaking I've done is since I retired in 2009 or 2010, since I met Al.

I learned a lot more about kayaking from Al and eventually took an instructor's course. Swiftwater rescue I did back in the '90s.

I've always been on the water, in a canoe or kayak or something, but Al's the granddaddy kayaker.

Al: I didn't start out in a kayak, though. I started canoeing when I was in high school, so that's what I did for many years. Then, one day, when I was living in Corvallis, I paddled my canoe upstream on the Willamette and the wind was coming up, and it was so strong that I had trouble getting back downriver again.

After that, I switched to a kayak, took a class from an instructor named Rob, who is the *real* grandpappy of kayaking in the valley, and it just sort of went from there.

Richard: I thought it was real neat that Travis contacted the two river guides in Eugene, but when they heard what Dean was going to do, they were very fearful.

Alice: They were not encouraging in the beginning.

Richard: No. They thought we didn't know what we were doing. Two people going down to Eugene and starting a month of travel? They just couldn't comprehend.

Alice: They had seen too many accidents. Too many drownings. They didn't know Dean could swim that well, so they just didn't trust Dean or Richard.

Al: Yes, we thought Dean was absolutely crazy at first.

Louis: Al and I discussed Dean's plans back and forth beforehand, wondering what experience he had swimming in a river and what experience he had swimming in whitewater. Did he know about the hazards along the river, like the strainers and the sweepers and the eighty-pound sturgeon lines hung up in the cold water?

Al: But Lou and I figured we'd give it a try and help Dean out, if we could.

Dean: The first time we met them, they put us in a drift boat and took us down the rapids. I think they wanted to scare us. The whole time they told us all sorts of tales about who had drowned in that portion of the river and when, you know, really trying to make us see how dangerous it was.

Al: The rapids on the Willamette are Class II, II+.

Louis: The I-5 rapids, before Alton Baker Park in Eugene, are very dangerous. A white water rafter with a lot of experience recently broke his shoulder on them and then, the December before last, a couple of stand up paddle boarders died when they hit a strainer going through there. That's where a lot of people get in trouble, because it's rocky, and if the water is low, it's not safe.

That was above where Dean put in, though.

Still, the Rose Garden Rapids, if you don't go through there the right way the consequences are serious. And then at Marist Rapids—you could call that Class II, II+—all kinds of things could go wrong. Concrete, rocks, foot entrapments, all kinds of things.

Richard: That first scouting trip with Al and Lou, both Dean and I were in the drift boat with one of them and the other was in a kayak ahead of us.

Alice: Al in the drift boat and Lou in the kayak?

Richard: Mmh-hmm. I think that's what it was.

Alice: Yeah, I'm pretty sure.

Dean: Lou was controlling the drift boat and Al was in a kayak in front of us.

Richard: I get 'em mixed up, Al and Lou, but anyway, I was in that drift boat, watching the guy watch Dean and me as we were going through the rapids. He said, "This is really dangerous here. This is where you're going to have trouble."

Dean: The drift boat was just rocking and going way up, then way back down, hitting hard. The whole time, I'm thinking, *I'm going to swim through this?* Of course, it was right after Lou had regaled us with stories of how many people had drowned there. I was kind of quietly panicking, but I didn't want to tell Dad.

Richard: Lou was checking body language as we went through these rapids, seeing if our eyes were popping out of our head.

Dean looked at me. I looked at him. We sort of laughed and said, "Piece of cake so far."

This guy had been on the river for many, many years and he must have thought he had two guys in his boat that were either completely insane or really didn't understand the problem. But we continued through a couple more rapids and when we were done they asked what we thought.

"I didn't see anything we couldn't handle," Dean said. "How about you, Dad?"

"No," I said. "We can handle that. I mean, we'll see what else is to come, but that didn't scare me. I've never been on a river like this, but I've been on a lot of mountains and have been a heck of a lot more scared on a mountain than I was on the river today."

Dean: I think Al and Lou expected us both to be pretty freaked out by the river, but I wasn't going to show anybody I was, and of course Richard Hall is not freaked out by anything.

But I remember talking to Dad later and telling him, privately, how skittish I was, how panicky I had felt as I was going up and down in that drift boat. I said, "Dad, what am I going to do?"

He said, "Just do it."

"What?"

"There's no way to know if you can do it unless you try," he said. "I don't think it's that big of a deal. We'll just do it."

"What about you in the kayak, though?" I asked. Dad had never really kayaked. Not through rapids, anyway.

He shrugged. "If I flip over, I flip over. No big deal."

I thought, *wow, I need a little more of the Richard Hall Attitude.*

Looking back, though, after having gone through what I did losing Mary, I was much more skittish in life. You know, something happened that I couldn't foresee and it changed my life forever. Dad really hadn't had too many of those experiences. I mean, he's had cancer three times, but he's powered through each one of 'em, so, I think he thinks he's invincible. At least he did at the time we were in the Willamette.

After that first run with Al and Lou, we talked to Travis. He said, "They want to do it again."

"That'd be great," Dad said.

"What?" I said. "No, we've already done the drift boat. We don't need to do that again."

"Why don't we get you down there and swim part of it?" Dad said.

"That sounds better."

Richard: I think Al and Lou decided we still did not understand the problem with that area of the river. They wanted us to come back again, probably to talk Dean out of swimming the Willamette altogether.

Dean: When we went back down for that final practice swim, it was an absolutely gorgeous spring day. The section of the river we chose to do was a little over eight miles and just south of Harrisburg. The river was narrow there, but fairly deep, and just this beautiful swirl of deep blues and greens. When I got in, I was glad I had my wetsuit because the water was ridiculously cold.

I took off so fast that Dad, Al, and Lou weren't ready and had a hard time catching up because the current was so swift. About five minutes in, I thought, *where is everybody?*

Finally, Dad caught up, but it took Al and Lou longer. I don't think they realized I could actually swim. Eventually, they went past us. By that time I was just starting to warm up, just starting to get going. Al pulled over on a gravel bar and motioned us all in with his paddle.

"What's going on?" I asked Dad.

"Al is motioning us in," Dad said.

"What for?"

"He wants to talk to you."

"Okay," I said, then swam over to shore.

Al looked at me and asked, "How are you doing?"

I said, "I'm fine."

"No," he said. "How are you *doing*?"

"I'm just warming up. Why?"

"We've almost gone a full mile."

"Yeah?" I said.

"We've gone a *mile*, Dean," he said. "Don't you need a break?"

"Al," I said. "I've got 187 miles I've got to do. One mile is a warmup. I'm just getting started. Let's keep going."

I got back in and kept swimming.

A while later, they all decided it was Lou's turn to be in front of me, but, as is typical with Lou, he got so excited he had them all paddling quite a ways ahead of me. I thought, *what are they doing way up there?*

They were all talking and not paying attention. Dad told me later both Al and Lou said to him, "Oh my gosh, we've never seen a swimmer like Dean."

Louis: I thought Dean was a very competent swimmer once I actually saw him in the water.

Richard: "Your son is something else to see swim," they said. "We've never seen a strong swimmer like that in our river, up here in Eugene. Most people say they're swimmers, but they're just in the water splashing around, but Dean swims so smooth and strong. The currents don't seem to bother him, either."

That's what they were worried about. Most of the people they'd tried to rescue didn't know how to handle the currents and were not as strong of swimmers as Dean. I think they were worried they would be rescuing both of us—me upside down in a kayak and Dean bumping along on the rapids.

Dean: I had the nicest swim that day.

It's sort of funny because I'm usually practicing mindfulness when I'm in the water, just being in the moment, but that day was so warm and the water was so clear and cold and fresh and I felt such a thrill from being alive and being in the Willamette, knowing I was going to do this thing, that I kept hearing some of my favorite songs. There's a Doobie Brothers song—"Black Water"—that I kept hearing it rolling through my head. That might have been the last time I heard a song in my head and swam to its beat, but it made the day really fun.

When we were about three miles from our ending point, I could tell we were getting close. The wind had died down so the water was super flat and calm. It was like swimming through glass and yet the current was still pushing me. That water was a deep, river-green—a kind of wild color—and every time I put my hand in the water I could see it ripple off my fingertips and the bubbles go by and I thought, *let's push the pace*. So, I just started cranking through this water. And in that moment, I felt so alive.

When I got out, Al and Lou looked at each other in disbelief and asked one another, "What just happened?"

Dean, cousin Wes, and Alice on top of Middle Sister in the Cascades, 1968.

Richard and Alice on a climb, 1954.

L to R: Richard, Lisa, brother Brian, and Dean hiking in the Cascades, circa 1972.

Dean's college soccer days in Kansas, 1979.

Dean and wife, Mary, 1980.

Mary, Dean, and Bre, 1993.

Dean post-swim, Kaw Lake, Oklahoma, 1995.

Bre, Dean, and Mary, Christmas, 2005, one year before Dean's first cancer diagnosis.

Dean, Mary, Bre, and dog, Beau, 2009—just one year before Mary's passing.

Mary and Dean, 2009.

Dean beginning to train in the pool, Fall 2013.

First trial run in the Willamette, no wetsuit, April 2014.

First swim in the Willamette with a wetsuit.

Richard during one of the practice runs.

Top Left: Richard, Dean, Kate, and Travis at Willamette Riverkeeper.

Above: Al Grapel paddling during a trial run.

Bottom Left: Al, Richard, and Louis on break during a second trial run.

PART II

"Miracles are here. Now, breathe them in. They long to be noticed and embraced."

~Mama River Whispers

FOUR

Dean: Growing up the son of two mountain climbers, I learned early on that what separated people who experienced mountaintops from those who did not was the courage to get out there in the first place and the strength that came with refusing to quit.

The same can be said about anything in life.

It's not about how smart you are, how talented you are, how brave. It's about how much you are willing to risk, and how long you can resist the urge to give up.

The first time I climbed Mt. Hood, Oregon's tallest mountain, I was ten-years-old. I was just this little guy, staring up at this huge mountain looming in front of me, getting ready to climb the whole thing with Mom and Dad. It wasn't technical by any means but it was such an overwhelming marathon to a little kid. As we climbed, I constantly thought I wouldn't be able to take one more step, but I didn't want to let down my parents or myself, because I really wanted to get to the top. I kept thinking, *I've come this far, why stop now?*

Somehow, I found a way to keep going and I was able to have that experience in early childhood of getting to stand on a mountaintop. I knew none of my friends had ever been up there and would probably never be. Looking back, I realize I didn't have anything extra or special about me other than the fact that I had the willpower to get up there.

That really made me believe that, if I put my mind to it and I was willing not to give up, I could do just about anything.

Thinking back on my dream to swim the entire length of the Willamette River, it seems incredibly silly that I wouldn't have second guessed myself. I had never swum anything longer than four or five miles in a river—and that was in the best conditions, in the warmest part of summer. I had never done any kind of marathon in a river. I was fifty-four-years-old. I had two types of cancer. But it honestly never occurred to me that I could not do it. That idea I'd had on the top of Mt. Hood had stuck with me, that all you needed to accomplish anything was the courage to dream and the willingness to pursue those dreams.

Bre: Dad is determined. He doesn't quit easily, or at all really. Growing up, I was taught that Halls don't quit. You are supposed to try your hardest to make something happen, to stick with it until there's absolutely nothing else you can do. So, I didn't doubt he'd try his best to swim that entire river.

Don't get me wrong, I was still nervous about him doing it. I didn't want anything bad to happen to him on the river. After losing my mom my greatest fear became losing him.

I think that's why I kept my distance from it all.

I tried to keep myself busy with work at the summer camp I counseled at so my imagination wouldn't race the whole time he was swimming, especially the first day when he was going through all of the rapids.

Lisa: Once Dean finally started the swim, I thought, *it's real. It's going to happen. He's actually doing this.*

Dean: Mom, Dad, and I got down to Eugene to the Comfort Inn, who had sponsored us, the day before the swim was supposed to start.

The first thing we did that evening was go down to take a look at the river so we would know exactly where we were going to put in the next morning. Kind of like a scouting mission.

The next morning, we got up and ate a nice breakfast. I was nervous, but not super jumpy. It felt like it was the same old same old, like we were going to do another practice swim. That's why I think it's so important when you're doing something like this to practice beforehand, because it's so hard anyway, right at the first, that if it feels familiar, then it makes it easier.

After breakfast, we went to Alton Baker Park where we were going to start. We had called all sorts of media stations beforehand and expected a lot of people to be there. I visualized the mayor of Eugene being there, maybe a brass band. *[Laughs]*. Yeah, there was nothing.

Richard: I was pretty excited about that first day. We didn't really know what we were getting into, but it seemed like it would be a great adventure. Adrenaline, of course, was going ten thousand miles an hour. It was good day.

Dean: When we showed up to the park, a man named Stephen Cridland was there. He was a photographer that had found out about us through Lisa's friend Mindy. He made his living photographing yachts. His photography is phenomenal so we were thrilled he wanted to join us on this venture and take as many photographs as he could.

Stephen Cridland (*photographer*): Getting involved with Dean's swim just seemed like a good thing to do. He was doing something that was really intense, and it didn't seem like anyone was thinking about the documentation end of it.

That's what I do. That's what I believe my position on the planet is. To record stuff, photographically.

Richard: We'd had a meeting with Stephen before the swim at a restaurant in Sellwood, just a meet and greet deal, and he seemed like a really nice guy who ended up taking some classic pictures of Dean.

Dean: I was thrilled we had somebody who was willing to take pictures.

Alice: Pictures at a professional level, too.

Dean: That first day, Stephen and Dad hit it off right off the bat.

Alice: Stephen was a friendly guy, and he talked to everybody.

Dean: But especially Dad. I thought, *hey, I'm the swimmer*, but Stephen was way more interested in talking to Dad, and I kept thinking, *he's going to want to start talking to me*.
  No, not so much. *[Laughs]*.
  Just Dad.
  They were joking and laughing. I thought, *how does Richard Hall do that?*

Richard: We talked about everything. Dean and the river. Pictures. What a journey we were on. He was very fascinated about somebody thinking about swimming the whole distance of the Willamette.

Stephen: I had never photographed something like that before. Not high adventure, anyway.
  I'm not an adventure shooter. My focus mostly is shooting architecture and interiors. I'm a slow shooter. My cameras are all wide lenses and I'm used to using a tripod. So, doing adventure photography is kind of a different thing for me and I find that exciting—to be able to do something different.
  Dean's quest had a lot to do with being on the water and the river, and I was really interested in the river as well.

Dean: As Dad and Stephen were talking, I sat on the back of Beowulf (Beowulf is the name I've given my 2007 Dodge

Nitro). I've got him geared up to look like he could go through a brick wall or withstand some kind of war. When I bought him in Tulsa, Oklahoma, I had them put on taillight guards, a roof rack, and a cattle guard in the front. They asked if I wanted anything else. I said, "How about gun turrets?" Because it we were in Oklahoma, they thought was really funny.

Anyway, so I sat on the back of Beowulf after we'd gotten the kayak down for Dad and I was putting my wetsuit on, quietly talking to Mom when Al and Lou showed up.

Lou was keyed up. Couldn't wait to get in the water.

Al was calmer. He took me aside and said, "Almost a year to the day one of the best athletes from University of Oregon drowned in the first rapids we are going to hit. Someone had thrown a grocery cart in the river and it had gotten wedged between some boulders. His foot got caught and he couldn't get out."

He had been talking pretty loudly, and I said, "Al, Al, Al, quiet down," because I didn't want Mom to hear.

Alice: I remember already being a little fearful for them, but I'm glad I hadn't heard that story.

Richard: It's a good thing I didn't hear it, either.

Alice: I remember Al and Lou both had said they'd rescued a lot of people out of there, but I know there were also a lot of people they weren't able to rescue.

Dean: Al said the other thing I'd have to watch out for were these limestone ridges in the first few miles. They have these tubular shapes and, if I wasn't careful and I hit a current, I could get sucked into one of the tubes. He said if that happened there'd be no way to find me again.

Right after he told me that, it was time for me to get in, but Stephen, who'd been taking pictures that whole time, said, "Stop."

"What?" I said.

"That's great light. Just stand there for a while."

Stephen: In that moment, he looked committed but also like he didn't really know what to expect.

Dean: I stood there for a while, and I didn't have anything else to do but think, Al's warnings swirling in my head. My thoughts start racing. *What have I gotten myself into? I'm here, I'm in the river, but I didn't swim for a year and a half to get ready for this. I haven't even been swimming for a full year. I'm still an active cancer patient. What am I doing?*

For the first time, I got the jitters about what I was doing.

I really started praying, asking for protection, for peace of mind, and, pretty soon, the jitters went away.

Even though the river was so cold, I just felt this warmth. I felt like I was doing what I needed to do and finally, since Mary had died, being who I needed to be.

When it was time, I dove in and the water felt so good.

It was a beautiful, clear day, even though it was a bit windy, and everything seemed like it was in high relief. It was one of those rare times in life where the greens seemed greener, the blues seemed bluer, and everything was just so gorgeous.

Richard: I had a rubber spray skirt around the top of the kayak to keep everything dry.

Louis: Before the swim even started, we talked about outfitting Richard's boat with a spray skirt to get through the rapids safely.

Richard: But I'm not even two strokes away from the park in calm waters and that thing *pewww!* Popped. And I thought, *this is not going to work. Going through rapids with an open cockpit?*

Louis: Without the spray skirt, he would have been swamped in those areas.

Richard: Right away, I pulled off to the shore and called— I can't even remember who I called, Dean or Lou— somebody and we got it fixed down tight.

Dean: I'd forgotten that. Dad called me over and I pulled it tight before I even dove in.
    But when I started to swim, my first thought was how crystal clear the water was. I could see the limestone ridges

Al had told me about, so as I'm swimming I'm watching these things carefully, just flying over them, but after about thirty minutes I realized there really wasn't anything to worry about.

Richard: I don't remember the limestone. That day, I didn't care about anything other than keeping my kayak upright.

Dean: Dad was the guide boater but he didn't care about the swimmer. *[Laughs]*.

Richard: The reason I didn't worry about Dean on that first leg was because Al and Lou were so concerned with watching him that I got the feeling they wanted to shepherd him along by themselves and have me keep out of the way. *[Laughs]*. They didn't say that, but I knew.

They were still very helpful with me. I had told them before, "I'm not a kayaker, and I've never done anything like this." So, they'd yell at me to go this way or that way. But it was about 99% focus on Dean and 1% on me.

Going through the rapids, I wasn't panicking. I thought, *this is fantastic. This is just a thrilling experience.* It was almost as fun as glissading down a mountain without skis or anything—you know, if the snow is just right, you come zinging down the side of the slope, but going through those rapids was a new experience. Just hitting those babies. *Bam, bam, bam.*

Alice: It was good practice for Richard, that first leg. Knowing that Al and Lou were going to save Dean if he needed saving, so he could get used to the kayak and the water before they were on their own.

Richard: Yeah, I didn't have to worry about Dean at all. All I had to do was remember to turn left or right and navigate down through the rapids. That's all I had to worry about—Dean who? *[Laughs]*.

Dean: I was concerned about Dad on that first set of rapids, because it had about four-foot rollers, but by the time I was just barely into the rapids he was already through it.

I could see him down in a little eddy, sitting and waiting with a grin from ear to ear, and so I thought, *this is going to be fun*.

But Al and Lou had me sit in the rescue position. It's classic when you're whitewater rafting and you're out of the boat. Put your feet forward and lean back. Very quickly I realized they'd never had anybody do that without a life jacket on.

I was hitting my tailbone on just about every boulder and I thought I was going to break it. I thought, *forty-five minutes into the first day and it's over*.

Louis: When you're in a defensive swim, your chin should be tucked and your butt up in the air. You don't want to stick your feet—whether you have a jacket on or not—up.

Dean: I think I had my chin too high and my feet too high.

Louis: Yeah, you don't want to do that.

But it's something you really need to practice in, say, swiftwater rescue classes. But if you went through some of those head-first, your noggin—that's what you'd be hitting.

Dean: Very quickly, I decided I'd better swim on my side.

I had barely switched positions when *wham!* I hit a boulder real hard. Right on my hip. I thought I'd broken it. Or cracked it, at least. That's how hard I hit.

I just kept going, because it was so loud and everyone else had flown by me in their kayaks, so there was nobody to tell. Then I thought if I hit that same hip again it would break if it wasn't broken already, so I flipped over to my other side.

Finally, the rapids subsided and I made it through. We came to an eddy and everybody asked me if I was alright, but of course, being a Hall man, I'm not going to tell them I'm doing badly. We decided to take our first break at this park just downriver. I swam there and my hip still really hurt. I could tell I already had a big goose egg on it and I was just wondering how bad it really was. I got out of the water and got Dad by himself.

"How you doing?" he asked.

"I think I really hurt myself," I said. "I'm up and I'm walking, so my hip isn't broken, but something happened."

"How bad?" he asked.

"I don't think it's too bad because I can put weight on it but look at my left hip." Even through the wetsuit he could see a big goose egg had formed.

"Oh my gosh," he said. "That doesn't look good."

"The nice thing is I'm using total immersion swimming," I said. "So I'm not kicking. All I have to do is drag that baby along behind me and the river's freezing so it will keep inflammation down. With fluid movement and cold that's better than any other situation so let's keep going and not tell Al and Lou I got hurt."

"Yeah," he said. "Why would we tell them?"

I kept going, but I had a goose egg for the first few days of the swim.

Stephen: I knew there wouldn't be a lot of rapids on the river, so I made sure to find the ones the guys would be moving through to take some shots. I actually walked through the water to get out onto an island where I figured they'd be coming through.

Dean: The picture Stephen took of Dad going through the first set of rapids is one of my favorites. His kayak is at this crazy angle and he's got this gigantic grin on his face.

Richard: Lou and Al explained that once we got through those rapids we could breathe easy, and that was really true, because once we got past the rapids we thought we were kings of the river. We had done *that*; what else could they throw at us?

The rest of that day was a fun trip floating down the river. Pretty good speed in the current, so I didn't have to paddle hardly at all. Just kept the kayak in the right spot and watched for Mr. Boy to make sure he was following me.

Dean: About thirty minutes after we were done with the rapids, I couldn't really feel the pain in my hip. Then, I got out of the river, warmed up, walked around a little bit and, man, it started to hurt again. I was bruised from my waist clear down my thigh. I quietly wondered if I would be taking shots like that every day. It freaked me out a bit. Then, I went to my old standby, my Alamo thought, as I call it. Whenever I'm feeling hard-pressed and worried about the next day or next few days I always tell myself, *yeah, it's hard. That's why nobody's ever done it.*

If you want to do something no one else has done, you've got to be willing to do what nobody else is. I thought to myself, *most people wouldn't be willing to take that kind of a shot and keep going.*

So, that's what I did. I kept going. The rest of the day was absolutely wonderful.

Richard: The first day was shorter than the others. Something like six miles. I did that on purpose because everything was still unknown. I didn't know how fast Mr. Boy would swim or what the speed of the river would be like. I was researching a subject I didn't know inside and out. I didn't know what we should be worried about. That first day, I knew I wanted us to get a taste for the water and what we're doing and not make Dean too tired.

Alice: Richard made that first day shorter so that they were sure to have success.

Dean: Having done that kind of thing so much in the wilderness, Dad knew if we started that first day feeling successful, then it would only build our confidence. Just getting started on such a massive adventure like that is so mentally draining that quick success almost determines ultimate success.

Richard: We stopped at Speedway, down by the Beltline Bridge. Looking back, I think that was a great first stop. Alice was there with the car, and we took out and congratulated each other.

Dean: When I got out of the river, I was tired but not too tired. Dad and I couldn't stop high-fiving each other. It was like we had won some kind of Olympic medal or something. Mom was there waiting, and she was so happy. She was cheering and grinning from ear to ear and Dad, in typical fashion, grabbed her and started kissing her.

    Stephen Cridland had beat us there so he could take a bunch of pictures of us coming in. One of them is probably my most embarrassing picture. I was trying to get out of the water, but I had my sandals on. They were rubber and these river rocks had a little bit of moss on them and were super slick, so I kept falling down. In this picture I've slipped and I'm trying to get up, but I can't and my nose is dripping and I look ridiculous and I'm on all fours. When I saw it I thought, *I hope that never gets published anywhere.* But I'm glad I have it now because everybody thinks doing something like what I did is just so much fun and so easy that they don't see the ugly, awkward moments—there are a lot of those.

It was so cold in the river that day that after I hugged Mom and stopped and stood and talked and laughed for a while, I quickly jumped into a hypothermic drop. So, I just started walking along the gravel bar along shore until Dad was done talking and we could put the kayak on top on Beowulf.

Dad was having such a good time talking to everyone. He just stood there for about thirty minutes chatting to Lou, Al, and Stephen.

That gave me time to reflect on the day. To think back on those first moments of my big adventure. Even though I took that hard shot and my hip was really hurting, I knew it was just a bruise. Nothing serious had happened that day. We had gotten through all of the rapids successfully. I knew from then on, most of the danger would be things like strainers and switchbacks and log jams. They were equally as terrifying, but a little easier to maneuver.

Richard: While Dean was walking around trying to warm up, I was talking to Al and Lou. What was interesting was the fact that they were only going to go that first day with us. Through the bad rapids. But they were so impressed by

Dean and what he planned to do that they said, "Would you guys mind if we tag along with you for the second day? Just go one more day with you?"

"If you've got time and you want to go along," I said. "We'd love to have you."

Alice: I think there was a lot of camaraderie among them when they'd stop. Al and Lou were having fun, you know, and Richard and Dean were having fun, too.

Richard: We all really connected.

Dean: I've found that when an adventure like swimming the Willamette really takes off, people who are involved get excited and want to play a bigger role. I think Al and Lou saw how unique my swim was and wanted to be a part of it for more than just a day. I couldn't have imagined a better group to spend those first days on the river with.

"Swim the river you're in.
Look only as far as the next riverbend.
Feel life;
laugh with me."

~Mama River Whispers

FIVE

Dean: The first time I got leukemia in 2006, I didn't suspect I even had cancer. It was only detected when I was going in for total-knee surgery and they had to do a blood test.

After the test, Dr. Watters came and met me at the office where I did therapy. He said, "Dean, sit down. There's something I've got to tell you."

We had become really good friends over the years. I was afraid he was going to tell me something bad about him, like he was getting a divorce or being sued—something like that. So, I said, "What can I do for you?"

"It's not what you can do for me, Dean," he said. "It's what I've got to tell you."

That's when I really started to worry, wondering if he was in real trouble in his life.

Then he told me I had cancer.

I don't know if I instantly went into shock, but my first thought was, *oh, good. He's all right.*

Then what he said sank in.

"I've got cancer?" I asked. "I've got leukemia?"

"Yeah, and it's bad, too," he said. "You have features of both chronic and acute. It's the worst-case scenario. I've made some calls to some oncologists, showed them your blood work, and none of them have ever seen anything like it."

"What's the prognosis?"

"If it doesn't change," he said, "weeks. Let's just hope and pray it changes, and when it does, let's hope for chronic. I've called an oncologist down in Ponca City, Oklahoma. I've got you an appointment at his office tomorrow."

After that, I started taking a blood test every two days. Thankfully, within about two and a half, three weeks it very clearly became Chronic Lymphocytic Leukemia or CLL. We breathed a sigh of relief it wasn't acute, but I was still one sick pup. I had no energy whatsoever. I was diagnosed four days before Christmas in 2006, and I was really sick for most of 2007.

I spent most of my time laying on the couch watching mindless reality TV shows I'd never watched or been interested before, which showed me how far I had slipped into the abyss.

The oncologist wanted to do some chemo and radiation, but I'd seen so many people that had done that as their first line of defense and then were stuck with hardened arteries and all sorts of physical ailments, so I didn't want that. I wanted to find a way to get better in a natural way that didn't have long term side effects.

The first thing I did was just a natural response. I had never really slept in my life. I'd always had two or more jobs, so if I got four or five hours of sleep, I was good. But I immediately started sleeping at least eight hours, many times ten hours, and I was so tired I would sleep all day, too.

Second thing I did was clean up my diet and not eat so much fast food, sugar, carbs, or highly processed foods.

The third thing I did, especially when things were pretty bad, was take liposheric Vitamin C. There'd been a lot of studies that showed Vitamin C killed cancer, but the problem with taking Vitamin C in a pill form is that it ruins your kidneys and liver, but there's a form that's semi-liquid called liposheric. I started taking it and that helped me quite a bit.

Finally, I started meditating two or three times a day, visualizing my body becoming strong and healthy and well.

By June of 2007, I was feeling considerably better. Then I got pneumonia.

It became so bad and my immune system was so weak that it almost killed me. I remember waking up in the hospital. Dr. Watters was standing over me with an IV and, as I opened my eyes, I was surprised I was in the hospital and then I was surprised at the look in his eyes—I knew him well enough to know he looked scared.

I said, "Hey, what's going on?"

"Oh, nothing," he said. "You just need a bit of extra fluid."

"No, Aaron," I said. "Tell me what's going on."

"As you know, you've got pneumonia and it's bad," he said. "You're really going to have to fight."

I thought, *okay, I can do that.*

Dr. Watters knew how clean my wife, Mary, kept the house and so he was pretty sure it was cleaner than the hospital, even though the hospital was very clean. So, he sent me home with my IV bag, several more, and a lot of medication.

From June of 2007 'til September I went through three or four rounds of steroids, and I just wasn't getting better. We were grasping at anything that could help. That's when Mary came up with the idea to get an electrical array footbath. When I heard about that I thought it was the dumbest thing I had ever heard of, but I was willing to try anything. So, I read through the information about this footbath. It said if it was lung problems the water would turn black. I thought, *pneumonia is obviously a lung problem, so let's see what this thing can do.*

I put my feet in the water and thirty minutes later this bath was just black. Thick as tar. I was shocked.

The treatment made me feel like I had the flu for a day or two after, but it said that could happen, and if you're really sick you should only do it every other day or every two days. So a couple of days later I did it again. Again, the water was black, but not quite as thick.

After about ten days of doing this footbath I noticed considerable results. My body was healing. So, I learned that there were natural ways, if I could just find them, to help assist my body to heal rather than look at traditional, prescriptive ways. That idea really helped me think outside the box the second time. It helped me realize the Willamette could help—mentally, of course, but physically as well.

Dr. Watters: As Dean progressed and started moving toward the river, we kept asking what if? What if? Because with a situation like his, where it's so unique, that's all we could ask.

What if?

Dean: Here I was, a cancer patient, swimming day after day in this wild river, but somehow I was never sore. I was never tired. I should say I was *tired*, but never to the point of exhaustion. Never to the point where I wanted to quit.

All my life, everyone that I loved had always told me I was the most stubborn person they'd met, and, usually, they said it in a manner of derision. Like it was a flaw. I learned, in the days before the swim and then especially those first few days on the river, that I could actually use my stubbornness as a gift. It didn't have to be a flaw in my character, but a strength.

Every morning at the hotel, when I'd come down to breakfast, I think Dad and Mom kept waiting for the day I'd say I didn't want to keep going. But I was so determined to swim the whole river and was so thrilled to be on an adventure in Oregon with my parents that quitting never crossed my mind. And that element of being with the two of them made it extra special.

Alice: We were all excited to just be together.

Dean: That first week, especially, was absolutely wonderful. The river was clean and beautiful. You know, growing up, the Willamette had been so polluted that it was hard to realize that it had been anything but a pristine, wild river. But it had been. When I was a kid I don't know if I would have even thought about getting into the river, at least not in Portland.

Travis: Everything from herbicides to industrial sites have polluted the Willamette, but over the past fifty years there's been a real effort to try and improve the Willamette River's condition. That applies to the habitat, which has certainly been a big issue, but water quality as well.

While Willamette Riverkeeper isn't the only group working to improve the conditions of the river, our effort is focused on addressing the public trust doctrine, which means the river belongs to everybody. It's not owned solely by a big industry or a powerful interest, even though at times it might seem like that. But that public trust doctrine really relates to, say, Dean's ability to access a river that should be clean, should be feasible for what he is doing and what other people are doing along that main stem, whether they're swimming, fishing, or camping along the river.

The Willamette should be healthy enough that they can be out there.

Richard: The river was beautiful the whole way down, but that first week especially.

What's sort of neat about following the river is that it puts you away from the industrial, away from the busy lives of everybody else. You're down in your little trough, in your own world—steep river banks, trees coming right down to the river—and it's real peaceful. Sitting in the kayak. Watching Mr. Boy swim. Nothing quite like it.

There were a lot of miles of nothing but peaceful river like that, but there were a lot of times where there were logistic problems. On our second day, as we were coming into—I forget where exactly. I'll have to look at a map—

Alice: —between Corvallis and Albany? No… *[Leaves the room quickly]*.

Richard: Anyway, they were doing construction on a new bridge. They had all these pylons in the river, making these swirls in the water. Lou and Al, of course, knew all about it. I think we could have gotten through there okay, but they stopped us beforehand and talked to us about how we should maneuver through that section.

Alice: *[Returns to the room with a map]*.

Dean: That was a dicey section of the river. There was a highway bridge that was fairly low and they were doing construction on it. They had this gigantic crane dropping five-ton pylons into the river right about where we were going through.

Al was worried, so we stopped and took a good look at what was ahead.

The river came down and bent to the right, then to the left, and then went through the bridge. But there was a huge kind of swirl that was shoving everything into the side of this construction site.

Al said, "Man, if you get caught up in that it won't be good. As soon as you get past that bend to the right and start going left, it will seem counterintuitive, but swim as hard as you possibly can straight left because that will keep you out of being pulled and stuck on the right and straight into construction."

Al: That's an interesting place. That river changes so much from year to year and there are places where the main channel was over here and now it's over here and cut off. The fact that it's gravel is what causes that to change so quickly. Now, if it was bedrock, like on the Umpqua River farther south near Roseburg, it would be different.

Louis: On that bridge, if you don't go through in the right spot, it doesn't matter if you're in a boat or swimming, you're not gonna make it out of there.

Richard: Because of the swirls in the water Dean would basically be swimming sideways. They told me the same thing.

"Get the kayak floating, but aimed at the center," they said. "Because if you don't do that it will throw you into the pylons, so you've got to fight it."

Dean said, "Yeah, okay."

Well he—

Alice: *[Taps finger on map]*. Was that near Harrisburg?

Richard: Yes. Harrisburg. That's it.

Anyway, we got through there no problem. Dean swam hard and in the kayak it wasn't too bad. I could feel the current pulling me toward the pylons but I just kept inching my way back toward the middle.

Once we made it through, Al and Lou just couldn't understand how Dean did such a good job on that. They didn't care about me—I thought I did an excellent job.

But we came through there and they said to Dean, "We never thought you'd be able to get through there. Never."

"No big deal," Dean said.

They were, all the time, just amazed at Dean's swimming ability. They kept telling me, "Geez, we've never seen anybody swim like that. Just his strength. His attitude about the water. His sensitivity about it. How he manages the current. He just seems like a fish in that water."

Al: After that, I think our concern shifted from Dean to Richard in the rec boat. He'd get pretty far behind, because he was constantly looking at the map to see where he was, I guess, and if he was really needed it would've taken a while for him to get there.

Richard: That second day was just like four little kids on a playground. We did a lot of bantering back and forth. Al giving Lou a bad time, Lou giving Al a bad time, and me giving them both a bad time and vice versa.

When the day was over, Al and Lou huddled together on shore for a little while. Then, they came over to us and said, "You know, we've been talking about it and we both can clear our schedule. Would you mind if we tag along with you guys for the rest of the week? We don't want to disturb you or change your program or anything else, but we'd really like to join you."

We laughed and told 'em absolutely. They were part of the party.

They were also a lot of fun to be around and we thought we'd take advantage of them while we could, what with their experience knowing the river as well as they did. They were not irritating to be around. They were fun guys, and, of course, Dean always kept things lively anyway.

Dean: That first week, we fell into a nice routine. Dad and I had done so many practice swims that we were kind of already in a rhythm as far as what we did with the kayak and everything else, and Mom and the guys easily fell into it with us.

I'd get up, make sure we had all of our gear, eat breakfast, go back to the hotel room, grab the gear, get to the car, drive to the river, meet up with Al and Lou, get in the river, and start swimming.

It was all very simple.

The one thing I always appreciated about that routine was that I never had to make any decisions. All I had to do was get my butt in the river and swim. Mom and Dad had everything else taken care of.

Alice: Well, Richard had everything taken care of. Every night after dinner we had to go to the store and get the next day's lunch, I remember that.

Richard: I would grab the munchables and some candy bars. A Boost drink for myself. It was really, if you think about it, a very mundane diet.

Alice: We made tea every day. Hot tea to warm Dean up.

Dean: The most challenging part about that first week came on day three.

We were going along just fine, then we hit a number of switchbacks and the water got shallower and shallower and faster and faster and then, the river just tumbled into this hairpin turn. On the far side of the hairpin was a big, nasty log jam.

Louis: The main problem on the Willamette after the rapids is not being able to see where to go. You could end up at a dead end in some bushes, you know, in a strainer or a sweeper. There's an old adage: rocks kill boats, wood kills people.

Most of the problems on this river are wood, you know, people getting caught in a strainer.

And on that hairpin turn, everything kind of goes right into that jam, so you have to stay on the inside of the curve.

Dean: Al thought I should go down one side and Lou thought I should go down the other side and Dad and I didn't know which way, so I was left trying to decide which way to hit this sharp turn on the fly. The whole time I was thinking about which way to go, the water was dragging me forward.

Pretty soon, I was not on one side or the other. I was in the very the middle of the river. The water was going so fast it started to roll me.

I rolled and rolled and rolled and was finally able to right myself just before I came up to the hairpin turn. I remember I dove over to the right side, which, of course, was going to take me right into that log jam.

There was no way to stop. I mean, the water was *moving*. I heard Al, who is normally Mr. Even, frantically yell, "Swim, Dean, swim!"

I swam for all I was worth, because I knew if I didn't the current would have pressed me against those logs with so much force I wouldn't have been able to get away and I would have drowned.

My heart was hammering, adrenaline racing, arms and legs pounding through the water. I barely skirted around the logs.

But once I was through I didn't breathe a sigh of relief, because, when I looked up, I saw we were coming up to another fast, shallow section of river. Dad was already moving through it, and his kayak was turned completely sideways.

Richard: I had been trying to watch Dean get past that log jam, then all of the sudden the river got shallow and I was scraping over the rocks. I thought, *okay, what do you do?*

I didn't want to turn the boat. I was afraid to do that. But then I had to have almost all of my weight on the left side so the water didn't come up over the gunwales of the kayak. So, I kept leaning and trying to paddle, while watching Dean at the same time and keeping an eye on the water, because I didn't want it to all of the sudden flip me—then I'd be in trouble. That was a real swift part of the river and I was not as strong of a swimmer as Dean.

I think Lou was over that way and Al was over that way and they were doing their thing and trying to talk to Dean as he got close to the log jam and I thought, *well, Dean, we're in this thing together, hopefully we'll come out on the other end.*

Dean: When I looked up and saw Dad, I thought, *oh my gosh, he's in trouble,* but he just looked a bit concerned, then he got a big smile on his face like he was having the time of his life. He kept going sideways until it dumped him into deeper water, then he went on like it was nobody's business.

We stopped very quickly after that and were talking about what had just happened and how scared we all were, but Al and Lou were the ones who were really scared. Maybe Dad and I were too stupid to be scared. We were talking mostly about what a great time we'd had and how it was such a shot of adrenaline.

Alice: Lou kept wanting Richard to just dive under and turn back over in the kayak. He wanted to teach him how to roll and get back up.

Richard: I said to him, "You're crazy."

Alice: Lou could do it.

Richard: Oh, yeah, he did it all the time just for kicks. *Pshht*—he's upside down and then pretty soon—*pshht*—he's back upright. He could do that so easily.

He kept telling me, "You're going to tip over one of these times, Richard, and you need to know how to flip back over."

"I'm not tipping over," I said. "I'm not going to get wet. I'm staying in this kayak, upright."

"No," he said. "You're going to tip over. One of these times, you'll get crossways with some real swift, shallow water. It's gonna flip you. Because once it goes over the gunwales, even a little water, it's game over."

I knew about water getting over the gunwales, because that's where Dean and his brother got into a problem when they were just kids coming down the Clackamas River. They wrapped their canoe around a rock. So, I knew how powerful the water could be.

But Lou kept saying, "You're going to go under."

"You're here to save me, then," I told him.

But, boy, he wanted me to tip over so bad.

Louis: I don't think I meant for him to learn to roll on that trip. Maybe I was trying to talk him into taking a class later.

Whether I had been serious about that or not I couldn't tell you. It was probably in jest, I would guess.

But it's been so long now I can't completely remember.

Richard: There were only a couple of scenarios where I came close to tipping, but for most of the trip it was just the old river pulling me along. It was such a joyful thing, me paddling, and every once in a while stopping to talk to Dean and telling him to look up at a plane that was doing some maneuvers or look over at some animal.

Dean: By the time we were getting close to Corvallis, which was about fifty miles into the swim, I was really feeling the energy of the river and realizing it was doing things to me I hadn't expected it to do.

There was a sense of peacefulness and relaxation I never assumed would be a part of that endeavor. I was doing it to raise money and inspire cancer patients by how hard it was and how that didn't stop me. And it was hard. Day after day after day I would get back to my hotel room, take a shower, and fall in bed for an hour before I could even eat dinner because I was so tired. So, it was definitely hard, but it was much more than that. It was fun, relaxing, enjoyable—I hadn't expected any of that. I just thought it would be insanely difficult and just a grind.

That day I swam into Corvallis, we weren't halfway into our first stint when Dad stopped me and said, "Hey, Dean, look at those."

There were two huge eagles, way up in a fir tree, roosted. Just standing there watching us.

Dad said, "They're probably wondering if you're a big fish and if they can take you out of the river and eat you."

We all laughed.

I kind of just floated for a while. As soon as I drifted by the eagles, they took off and started circling me. They did that the whole time I was swimming. Then, we got to the next place we were breaking at, and I stopped. Got out of the water.

Al said, "Look at that."

Those two eagles had stopped and perched in a tree just across the river bank.

Richard: We would start up and they would fly along with us until we stopped for a break, then they would stop, too. When we would start up again, we'd look up and there they were, flying.

Dean: That whole leg of the swim, all the way into Corvallis, whenever I would stop, those eagles would stop. Whenever I swam, they'd circle over us.

I kept thinking, *well, this is strange, because we're hours into this thing and they're still with us*. I kept thinking at any time they would fly off, but they didn't.

When we stopped for the day, they stopped. Dad and I started to pack up the kayak and they just sat there. A reporter from the local newspaper came to interview me and they were still sitting in the tree until finally, toward the end of the interview, I guess they realized we were done swimming and they flew off.

Al had been talking for days about Native Americans and their connections to eagles. He said when eagles circle you it's a sign of destiny, of blessing. He said, "That's the coolest thing I've ever seen, and I've seen a lot of things on the river in my years. I just look forward to see what's going to happen to you next."

Al: I guess I don't remember the eagles.

Dean: It was one of the most interesting experiences I've ever had. That's what adventure does, though. It gives you the bumps and bruises, but it also gives you some of the most unexpected gifts you'll ever receive.

*"My water comes from everywhere.
My water is your water—
you are water."*

~Mama River Whispers

SIX

Travis: I don't think a lot of people think about the Willamette for recreation, but if I was living in Albany or Corvallis, I would think about it constantly, because there are so many good places you can go on that stretch of river.

Louis: You ask what brings me back to the river? Easy: the river.

Al: There's something about being in a boat. It's not like land where it's *plod, plod, plod.* In a boat, there's so much motion, all the time. And different kinds of motion, too.

A river is better for me than, say, a lake.

Why?

Because it's alive.

Louis: Once you get to Eugene and beyond, you're in a floodplain, so you're basically in a wilderness. You can see beaver, you can see bears, you can see eagles, you can see fish jump.

One of the things that Al and people we paddle with are always saying is "where is everybody?"

Ninety percent of the time we're the only people on the water because the hot weather's gone and we paddle—rain, snow, it doesn't matter.

Where are all the people?

Alice: It's probably the quietest area, between Corvallis and Salem. It's where most of the farms are—well, there are farms all along the way, but there aren't really any towns up there. No people, really. Just cows.

Richard: That reminds me—back in the 70s, Alice, Lisa, and I took our canoe from Eugene to Independence. We camped along the side of the river bank on this sort of a sandy area and we woke up early in the morning to this sound. *Thump, thump, thump, thump, t-t-t-t-t-thump.*

I looked out of the tent, thinking, *what in the world is going on?* Well, the noise was from the cows coming down to the river, and our tent was sitting right in their path.

So, yeah, there are cows along the river and they're very interesting, but the section from Corvallis to Salem is just sort of quiet, tranquil. Dean was able to stretch out his strokes and really do some swimming.

Dean: Once we got past Corvallis it really felt like we were in the heart of the Willamette Valley. Typically, one side of the river bank would be forested or heavily wooded and the other side would just be rolling hills and farmlands. I very rarely heard any kind of road noise or saw any people. Just big Douglas Firs. Fast-moving water going this way and that. It was like we were in some kind of National Park. Down there, it was just wild riverbanks.

Even though we were in this secluded, gorgeous area, the first day without Al and Lou was hard. Both Dad and I missed their company, and it was difficult to slip back into the pattern of it being just the two of us. Al and Lou's absence was very noticeable, on top of the rain setting in.

So, we were alone, it was dark and rainy, and then we hit this dead zone where it seemed like no one else but us cared what we were doing. We tried to get some press coverage. We contacted the newspapers in Albany and Salem. They didn't even call us back.

By then, the newness of this adventure had worn off and we hit that weird mid-stage where it felt like we'd always been on the river and like we might *always* be on the river. Like there was no end in sight.

Richard: I never felt that way—like there was no foreseeable end. I focused on the river one chunk at a time. From Eugene to Corvallis. From Corvallis to Salem. From Salem to Portland and so on. I had my own vision of getting to the Columbia River and, at the time, I was very confident we—

Alice: They didn't know about the Newberg pool yet.

Richard: No, no. Didn't know about that. Still, I was very confident we would make it to the finish line, unless Dean ended up with an injury of some kind.

Dean: I remember one time, not too far past Corvallis—well, to put it in context you need to know Dad didn't have a phone with GPS, so he was constantly studying the map Travis had given us. Anyway, one time when Dad was looking at the map he had forgotten I was following behind him. *Bam.* I swam right into the back of the kayak. My goggles bashed against that hard plastic. I don't think it actually cut me, but it did not feel good. I was so frustrated, but I knew that if I started yelling at Richard Hall it wouldn't go well. So, I put my head down in the water and cussed a blue streak for about three or four minutes. I was saying all sorts of terrible things as I swam. Then, finally I came up for air.

"Hey, how close are we to taking a break?" I asked.

Dad didn't answer my question. He just looked at me. "Are you done?"

"Done with what?"

"Couldn't exactly hear what you were saying," he said, "but there were some pretty loud bubbles coming out of the water back there."

That was about as close to any kind of tiff we ever had. More often than not we had this wonderful synchronicity. We were having our own, separate adventures—Dad in the kayak, me in the water—but relying on each other at the same time.

Dad totally took care of me throughout the swim. We'd stop, he'd throw my sandals to me. I'd put them on and wander to shore. He'd drop me in a space blanket and put a beanie on my head, because whenever I got out of the river I was always shivering uncontrollably since the water was so cold. Then, Dad would hand me things to eat and give me hot tea. To say it out loud, he sounded like my personal valet. *[Laughs]*. But it was just fun to be doing what I loved with my dad by my side. We experienced so much together during that time.

When we were coming out of Albany, north of Corvallis, Dad stopped me.

"Hey, look at this," he said.

There was a red biplane doing all sorts of crazy barrel rolls and loop de loops and then—I think it's called a hammerhead or a tomahawk, where they go straight up until they lose all of their momentum and just hang there before they start falling backward, then point their nose down. This guy did that several times. We drifted in the water for about five minutes while we watched this plane.

We had little, unexpected moments like that time and time again. Yeah...just little gifts from the river.

Alice: But the journey wasn't without its dangers.

There was one time there was an island in the middle of the river and Dean headed to the right and Richard headed to the left.

Richard: That's the only time I was very fearful.

Alice: Because the current was going so fast.

Richard: Yes, it was moving so swiftly, and I thought we had communicated that we would go left of the island.

Dean: The closer we got this split, the more and more shallow the river became, and the current was going faster and faster and faster and pretty soon it's only inches deep.

Richard: Dean got into that current, moving to the right, and I was too far ahead, going left.

Dean: I swam as hard as I could to try and go left, but couldn't do much of anything because I was in such swift, shallow water. The river started taking me to the right side of the island. Finally I yelled, "I'm going right."

As soon as I said that, the current started rolling me shoulder over shoulder until I hit a couple deep holes. Then, I started going end over end, really becoming disoriented.

Richard: I beached my kayak as fast as I could and ran across that rocky island yelling, "Dean, Dean," in as loud a voice as I could, but the river was so loud, it drowned me out I think, because I didn't hear a reply. I couldn't see him anywhere. I thought, *where is he going to end up? Is he going to go beyond the island? Is he going to stop somewhere on the island? How are we going to match up again? Is he going to be all right?*

Dean: I'd been rolled so many times and in so many different ways it took me a while to reorient myself.

Finally, the river got deeper and the current calmed a bit, so I swam over to the island and sat down on this big boulder. I felt so dizzy and was just about ready to get up when Dad came running over.

Richard: I was very happy to see the big stud out of the water.

Dean: I walked back to where his kayak was and sat down.

And I shouldn't have sat down.

I had gotten rolled so many times and was so cold and it had just started to rain like crazy that the combination of all of that shocked me and I immediately when into deep-core hypothermia. We still had three or four miles left for the day, but I went into this terrible daze.

"Do you wanna call it?" Dad asked. "We're in farmland. I could just crawl up this bank, walk through some fields, and try to call your mom."

"No, we're not gonna do that," I said. "I *am* cold though and need to get warm."

"Let's make a cocoon, then."

Dad took the space blanket we had and wrapped it tightly around my body, holding it around my head. I could hear the rain beating against the outside of the blanket, but I couldn't feel it, because he was holding it so tight.

It took me a while to get warm.

"Are you ready to go on, now?" Dad asked.

"No," I said. "It feels really good in here."

"Well, you can't stay in there forever."

"I know," I said. "Just give me a little bit longer."

He gave me another minute or two, then asked, "Are you ready?"

"Tell you what," I said. "How about you count me down."

"What?"

"Count me down and I'll be fine."

He sort of laughed, then started counting. "Ten, nine, eight…"

Finally, when the cocoon opened up on the count of one, I got hit with this cold blast of rain-soaked air, but I managed to get back into the river and had a pretty nice swim for the rest of the time.

The rain cleared and, about half a mile from Independence, our stopping point for the day, the river started going a little faster, making it easier to swim.

When we reached the boat ramp at the park in Independence, I saw Mom's brother, my uncle David, sitting there with a goofy grin on his face, giggling—of course. He was always giggling. He had a map in his hands and was trying to figure out where we'd been and where we were going. I thought when I saw him he'd congratulate me, or talk about what a feat it was to swim all the way from Eugene to Independence, or comment on how incredibly brave I was, or say something about my athletic prowess.

Nope.

A retired teacher with a deep hunger for learning and one of the most inquisitive minds I had ever known, the only thing ole Uncle David was interested in was the Willamette itself. Wanting to know what each area looked like from down in the river and how far it was from this point to that point and how long it took me. I thought, *oh, of course this is what Uncle David would talk about.* He was constantly curious about little details 'cause that's the way his mind worked. So, I just laughed, put my ego in check and gave him all the facts, because he was so fascinated by it all.

Richard: It was thrilling to come into Independence, because it wasn't too far from there to Salem, the state's capital.

We saw Salem as this great destination point, because we felt like if we made it to Salem, it was all sort of downhill from there. Nothing could stop us. The rest of the river was within our grasp.

Dean: Salem was the 100-mile mark of a 187-mile swim.

That's when I started gaining confidence, because, for months, I had visualized swimming into Salem. I believe visualization is an important part of cancer recovery, or accomplishing any dream, really. So, every night, I would envision starting in Eugene and swimming into Salem triumphantly, then I'd picture myself swimming straight in the Columbia River.

As soon as I swam into Salem, however, I realized I hadn't visualized swimming out of Salem. I had visualized swimming into Salem and swimming into the Columbia River and I thought, *there's a long distance between those two.*

Apart from the few practice swims Dad and I had done closer to Portland, I wasn't really sure what to expect or what the river would hold. In my mind, it all seemed very unknown.

"Feel life everywhere. Hear my song. Sing with me, dance with me, swim in me."

~Mama River Whispers

SEVEN

Dean: Swimming out of Salem was a turning point in the whole swim. It was a Saturday. Several members of my extended family were there, as well as my daughter, Bre.

Lisa: As Dean and Dad got closer to Portland, my husband Steve and I would try to see them when we could. We were there that day in Salem.

I loved seeing Mom on the dock supporting them. That kind of familial tenderness between all of them was present between all of them, but the bond between Dean and Dad at that time was just super special to watch.

Dean: It was odd to have more than just Mom and Dad there in Salem that day. My family had seen me go through so much and then probably thought I had completely lost my mind trying to swim the entire Willamette, so it was nice having them there to support me.

Bre and I fell into our typical banter. Laughing, talking, sharing lines from our favorite movies.

Bre: Dad and I have what we call the "Dean and Bre list" of favorite movies. Basically, they are the films we could watch over and over again together and quote from for hours on end.

Dean: *What About Bob, Remember the Titans.*

Bre: *School of Rock, A League of their Own.*

Dean: *Ferris Bueller's Day Off.*

Bre: *Lawless.*
That's just to name a few.

Dean: I was really happy to have Bre there that day in Salem. We were having fun, sure, but I truly hoped she would see that I was not insane, but inspired. I hoped that she would understand that, while I told everyone I was doing the swim to raise money for cancer research, or to inspire other cancer patients to never give up, I was also secretly and more importantly doing it to convince her that she was not going to lose her second parent before she turned twenty-five.

With all of my heart I hoped my real self would show through enough that she would see me, not as the confused, broken man shattered by sadness she couldn't count on, but as the strong father figure I had tried to be when she was young. I wanted to earn the right to be Bre's highly-respected and greatly-beloved father again.

It was a secret I would never tell anyone. Not even Bre, until years later.

Bre: I don't remember thinking anything brilliant or profound about Dad while he was swimming the river. Like he was returning to his old self or anything of the sort. Those thoughts came later.

I was so numbed out by my own grief that summer, it was all I could do just to show up and observe and force myself to participate in "typical" conversation.

And sometimes, I couldn't even do that.

Dean: I think I was scaring the shit out of Bre and didn't even know that I was. I think that's why she kept her distance.

Bre: I don't think that's why I stayed away. Honestly—and I don't talk about this at all—there were some days, when I wasn't working at camp, all I would do was lay on the floor of my room and stare at the wall. It felt like my grief was weighing me down, keeping me on the floor. I missed my mom more than I could ever admit out loud, and I spent hours wishing I had one more day with her, just one. Then, I spent many more hours getting slapped in the face over and over again by reality: I would never get one more day, one more hour, one more minute. I wouldn't even get a single second more.

And, usually, when I reached that point in the tirade of thoughts, I knew I'd better stay on the floor and stare at the wall, because if I got up I was going to do something to harm myself.

Dean: Wow, I didn't know about that at all.

Bre: I didn't tell anyone how badly I was struggling, and by then I'd had a lot of practice putting on a 'happy face' in front of other people, so I don't think anyone really suspected.

Looking back I see how bad of an idea it was—to keep my struggles to myself. So that summer was really difficult for me. Half of it I was in a fog and half of it I was just trying to keep myself alive.

I showed up to what I could of Dad's swim and, looking back, I'm really glad I was there that day in Salem.

Dean: As I swam out of Salem, I was celebrating.

I was halfway there.

The seemingly scary portions of the river were behind us.

All I had to do was put my head down and keep swimming. All I had to do was finish the damn thing.

Bre: I do remember that watching Dad swim out of Salem was mesmerizing.

I'd watched him swim across lakes and in pools my entire life, but seeing him on the river was something else entirely.

He was—and I can already hear the protests and guffaws he'll make when I say this—graceful. His arms reminded me more of birdwings than anything. Bent and ticking in and out of the water in long, even movements that just made him glide.

It looked effortless.

Dean: As I took my first strokes and aimed at the middle of the river to catch the current, I vowed I would finish the swim. Even if I was so broken I had to swim with one arm I would finish. I would finish no matter what.

I glanced up at the railroad bridge briefly as I turned my body to the north and was quickly caught up in the current.

Suddenly, the river ceased to be the wild place we were accustomed to, and we moved through a stretch of immaculately-manicured riverbanks, beautifully-appointed houses, and highly-landscaped lawns reaching down to well-maintained docks and boat launches.

Then, for the first time, we were passed by a speedboat towing a water skier. Both the driver and the skier looked at us with a mix of curiosity and disdain. Like we were in their way.

Richard: After we left Salem, we started to see more and more boaters running around. So they'd know there was a swimmer in the water, I had an orange flag, and every time I'd see a boat I waved the flag. They would give us a wide berth, but not too many of 'em slowed down. And that sort of ticked me off, because we'd hit their wake and things would get screwy for a while.

Dean: By that point, I had such a deep connection to the Willamette I'd started referring to it as Mama River. It's hard to explain to people who have never felt a strong tether to nature, but at times I could almost hear the water and her comforting words whispering to me. And when the speedboats would pass, just ripping up the river while those on board drank their beers and cranked their music, I could taste traces of gasoline in the water, and it made me a little angry at how flippant they were and how disrespectful they were being to nature.

I believe our rejection of that ancient calling to be a part of nature rather than separate from is the reason we have so much pollution now. Because, rather than see Mother Nature as a mother who gives us sustenance and life, we consume its resources or see it as a terrifying enemy that needs to be destroyed or like it's a great amusement park for us to play on.

And nature is none of those things.

Nature is a living, breathing variety of beings, much like ourselves.

It's important to note, I did not think this way before the swim. I learned these things on the river. Even entering the swim up in Eugene, I saw the Willamette as kind of a racetrack I was going down in order to accomplish this great feat. I think I had often seen nature as my playground, and I was still largely in that mindset for most of the swim.

Then, I started to feel its power and its movement and see its personality. I started to learn from it. The very way the water was moving and flowing taught me so much. I realized I had spent my entire life seeing obstacles in my path as something I needed to dominate or move or crush. Water didn't do any of that. It never fought anything as it flowed. It didn't waste its energy. It just moved around, over, and through without any need for conflict or violence.

So it's those kinds of little things that started to change the way I looked at the river and the way we all view nature.

Once Dad and I started to see speedboats and water-skiers all the time, it made me long for Mama River's wilder ways.

Richard: But, you know, people are people. They're going to do what they're going to do. Thankfully, we never had any close calls with those speedboats that I remember 'cause I was pretty vocal, too.

"Hey, there," I'd shout. "Whoa."

Alice: They had the ferries that shuttle cars across the river to deal with after Salem, too. Wheatland Ferry north of Salem and then one further on in Canby.

Richard: Crossing with the ferry wasn't a scary deal, because we could see them quite a ways ahead. To me, they were just another logistic to figure out.

The biggest concern was that the ferries on the Willamette move back and forth on these cables and we didn't want a tight cable screwing around with Mr. Boy's body.

Dean: The cables extended from bank to bank and were pretty close to the surface. I didn't know if they were conducting electricity or not, but I had all sorts of wild imaginings about getting zapped or at least tangled up in them.

Richard: We had to time it just right to avoid these things. That meant if Dean had to swim fast, he swam fast, and if he had to float and smoke a cigar while he waited, then he did that. *[Laughs]*.

Dean: I never *did* have time to smoke a cigar, and, in actuality, those cables I was so worried about were about six to ten feet underneath me.

Richard: We tried to time it just right, but if we got there too early, we would slow it down, wait.

Dean: We would just float for a little bit.

Richard: And when we'd see them take off we'd—*BAM*—plow ahead.

It worked out real well.

There were a few other logistical issues, one being an access point we really needed.

Dean: There was one stretch of my swim between Salem and Newberg that was going to be twenty-three miles long.

Richard: Way before Dean and I ever got on the Willamette, I was telling a friend of mine that there was a portion of the river where there was no boat ramp, no place to land.

He said, "Where is it?"

"Near Dayton," I said.

"Well, I know the pastor of a church out there," he said. "I'll give him a call and see what I can do to help."

So, he called and the pastor was very excited about what we were doing and, boy, did he jump on that thing. He hunted all over.

Dean: He found a farmer who had acreage that butted up to the river and was willing to let us onto his property. That cut the twenty-three miles roughly into half.

Richard: But this was no picturesque park. It was some God-forsaken, ugly place to land.

Alice: Nothing but a muddy field.

Richard: Terrible place.

Alice: And the river was a long ways from the main road. I had to drive down this old farm road, and it was nothing but mud.

Dean: The road that went down to the river skirted this farmer's orchard area and then took a bend north and went way down and way up two or three times, and in the bottom of these gullies were just huge washouts from the rain. Lots of mud. Mom had to pick us up from there and drive that road on her own in Beowulf in four-wheel-drive.

Dad and I were sure Mom wouldn't be there because she would get stuck in the mud.

Not only was she there, but she was grinning from ear to ear.

"How was the muddy road?" I asked her.

"It was kind of bad," she said. "But it was also kind of exhilarating."

Alice: Only Dean's car would have been able to get through. I wouldn't have wanted to drive my car, that's for sure.

Richard: But despite all the mud, it was someplace, at least. An intervening place that meant we didn't have to just chug on by and wear Dean out. I appreciated that.

Dean: That stretch of the river seemed to be filled with one incident after another.

Alice: I remember the next day they passed through St. Paul. Dean was almost dangerously hypothermic.

Dean: We weren't supposed to end at St. Paul that day. We just saw Mom there on one of our breaks and stopped for a little while.

Alice: Dean stopped and I turned the heater on full blast in his car and he sat in there for twenty or thirty minutes.

Dean: That was our long, fourteen mile day. I was tired.

Alice: Tired and cold.

Dean: We had done a ten or a twelve miler the day before. Ten the day before that. Twelve the day before that. We had done some heavy miles before that fourteen mile day. Then, to add insult to injury, it was raining, which only made it colder.

Alice: The sky was dark. Thick clouds just hanging ominously above us.

Dean: When I got into the car at St. Paul, I was tired and ready to be done, but I knew I had to make it into Newberg. That was still another four miles away.

Alice: That was such a hard day. I think Richard had called from the river and asked me to find something hot for Dean to drink, so I found some tea.

Dean: I'd forgotten Mom did that.

Alice: It helped warm Dean up somewhat, but he still had to get back in the cold river and rain right after, so I'm not sure what good it really did.

Richard: About that same time, we were getting closer and closer to Newberg. The current started to slow down. For the first time, we didn't have the push of a strong current. Time seemed to stretch. Like we were making no progress. All in all, it made for a very long day.

Dean: The day I finished in Newberg I was exhausted.

Stephen Cridland, the photographer, was with us, because I remember I had him take pictures of my hands, because, even after having been out of the water for thirty minutes or so, my hands were still kind of blue and purple. It really didn't show up in the picture but it was still kind of alarming.

Stephen: That wasn't me, I don't think. Did I meet them in Newberg? I don't know, maybe I did. If I took the picture, I've got it somewhere, because I have all the photos on a hard drive.

So, no I don't remember taking that specific picture, but I do remember Dean being cold...a lot.

Richard: That night, we had planned to meet up with Alice's and my financial advisor, Todd, who lives in Newberg, for dinner. It was supposed to be this small gathering, a party, and Dean was hopefully going to do a little fundraising with them.

I had to call Todd and say, "Hey, I am terribly sorry, but Dean is nothing but a wet noodle. He doesn't have any energy, so we are gonna feed him and put him to bed."

Still not sure what Todd said to all those people planning to come and celebrate Dean. I'm sure they had a great time without us there. Alice and I could have gone, but it didn't feel right going and representing Dean without him, because it would have been a big letdown to all of them, I'm sure; but they were generous enough that they still gave quite a bit of money to the Leukemia and Lymphoma Society.

Dean: We got to the hotel in Newberg and I had my wetsuit stripped down to my waist and I'm muddy and still a little purple. I went to push the door open to the lobby and the muscles in my shoulder and upper arm were so tired that the door didn't even budge. I ended up falling into it and landing on the floor in the middle of the lobby.

The people who worked the front desk didn't even look up. I don't know how they missed me falling through the door, but I was almost glad they hadn't seen me.

Dad came in after me, and I was still lying there, too tired to get up.

"What's going on?" he said.

"I'm too tired to get up."

"Well, you're going to have to get up."

"Could you help me?"

He gave me a hand, and I stumbled up to my room, took a shower, and went to sleep immediately. It was only about six o'clock.

But the next day, I woke up feeling refreshed. As I sat on the edge of the dock at Roger's Landing in Newberg, I couldn't help but notice how lustrous the river looked. The sun was out and reflecting off the water. Mama River shimmered up at me, as if she was saying hello. Calling me back, ready to play.

Dad got into his kayak and paddled past. I jumped in.

The water felt cold and fresh. It quickly swept away any of the cobwebs that remained from the previous day. I was upbeat. I thought that stretch of water would be an easy, eleven-mile push into Wilsonville.

By the time I took my second stroke, I knew I was wrong—dead wrong.

Travis: That portion of the river is known as the Newberg Pool.

Dean: It gets deep and wide for a few miles right along that stretch.

Richard: I think of it more like a lake than a river at that point.

Travis: There's not a lot of current and, especially if a summer wind comes up, you could be out there slogging along and still feel like you're just sort of crawling.

Then the challenge becomes mental.

You know, what progress have you made? How do you stay upbeat? I think that's like anything, though, whether you're running or swimming or doing a long distance hike. I think that slow, ticking away, especially if you're starting to feel a little tired, becomes a mental battle very quickly.

Dean: I was making the same motions that I always did, finding the same rhythm, but I wasn't moving at the same rate. Not even close. I was almost dead in the water. Nothing left in the tank.

I thought, *this is going to be a long day*.

Richard: With no current at all, Dean's having to swim every single inch of the river. He didn't get any kind of assist at all.

He was really having trouble staying focused on just swimming.

I remember there was this bridge just downriver from Roger's Landing there in Newberg.

Dean: I was using this bridge to track my progress.

Richard: He kept looking up. And then swim, swim, swim. Look up again. Swim.

Dean: Finally, I'm moving under the bridge, and I thought, *good. Now I'm getting somewhere.*

I knew all I had to do was keep swimming and, before long, that stinkin' bridge would be nothing but a tiny blip behind me.

This became my mantra: Stroke, bridge, stroke, tiny, stroke, blip. Bridge, stroke, tiny, stroke, blip.

It sounds almost stupid that a mental chant could spur me on, but I'd been swimming for weeks, still had weeks left to go, and I was doing what I could just to keep moving.

Richard: But he'd look back at the bridge and it would still be the same distance away.

Dean: Despite my sing-song repetition, my 'tiny blip' of a bridge seemed as if it was still right above me, almost sneering at my lack of progress. I stopped. My hand curled into a fist.

I don't know if I was too exhausted or too far inside my own head or what, but I was getting ready to shake my fist at that bridge and tell it what for.

Then Dad interrupted my swimming-induced insanity with a shout.

"Hey." He was twisted around in his kayak further downstream. "What are you doing?"

"I thought I'd gone much farther."

"You're not moving too fast today," he said, and I knew he was holding back a little. You know, being nice. "Just keep swimming and you'll be fine."

"I'm not going to be fine until I can't see that stinkin' bridge anymore."

"Then you better get going." And with that Dad turned his kayak back around and started paddling away from me.

Richard: We had to stop quite a few times for Dean to rest that day, even though most of the docks were private. You know, violators will be shot signs or something like that. *Screw 'em*, I thought. Dean needed to get out of the water. So, I just started picking the private docks out that had ladders so it'd be easier for him to climb up.

Dean: The odd thing about that stretch of river was there was hardly a river bank. The trees came right down to the water, and instead of the tall pine and cedar we'd been seeing, it was more oak and elm. They were so tightly packed and their canopies so thick I couldn't see anything past them. So, we were down in this slow-moving, green river, nothing but trees all around, no breeze. It felt almost claustrophobic. And that didn't help the fact that I had nothing in the tank as far as energy.

Richard: I could tell he wasn't swimming like he normally did. His strokes were just not as crisp and powerful as they usually were. It was probably the worst day for Dean, the whole swim, that leg outta Newberg. A real Bataan Death March.

Dean: I didn't end up making it all the way to Wilsonville that day.

Richard: He kept at it for about seven miles until we reached Butteville. Little community.

We came into that area, and there were some beautiful docks there. I saw some houses up on the hill, and Dean was doing so bad, I thought, *this is it, this is where he's got to stop for the day.*

So, I picked out a dock. Pulled over to it.

Dean said, "What are we doing?"

"Getting your butt out of the water. You don't have anything left, Dean."

He was so exhausted he couldn't argue.

Alice: He was so tired he had a hard time getting up onto the dock, if I recall.

Richard: He finally rolled up there like a walrus or something. Flopped there.

Dean: Dad kept referring to me as the dead seal on the deck.

Richard: I thought we would probably have to try and find somebody who had blankets and a pillow, because he was going to stay the night.

Then, the guy who owned the house came down and asked, "What's going on?"

"My son is swimming from Eugene to the Columbia River," I said, "and this was not a point that we wanted to stop, but he's so exhausted, this is it for today."

Dean: I was laying there and Dad said, "Dean, introduce yourself."

All I could do was raise one hand up to this guy. I didn't even lean up because I was so tired. Finally, after about thirty, forty-five minutes, Dad helped me up off the deck.

Richard: Dean said, "Well, what do we do now?"

"Butteville's not that far away," I said. "I'll walk in and try to get cell phone reception to call your mom."

"Well, I'll go with you."

"Are you sure? Look at those steps up there."

Long steps up to the road. He looked. Looked back at me.

"Yeah, I'm going with you," he said.

So we walked up those long stairs and got to the road.

Dean: I wandered through this guy's yard and, having been in Butteville so many times, I knew where we were, so I started walking to the Butteville Store. I kept asking Dad, "Have you called Mom, where's Mom?"

Finally, he said, "I can't get ahold of her she's not answering her phone."

Alice: There wasn't any cell service, and, you know, how would they connect with me? Because Butteville was not on our radar for meeting up. Not even as a stopping point along the way.

Dean: Dad just started screaming, "Aliiice."

Richard: "Aliiice."

Dean: "Aliiice."

Richard: You know, my brain is in upside down and backwards.

Dean: I said to him, "She's not in Butteville. She can't hear you."

Richard: "Oh, yeah? Yeah?" You know, challenging him. Then, pretty soon, about two blocks down, she came around the corner.

Dean: When I saw her, I said, "Oh my gosh that worked."

Richard: We thought, *this has got to be some kind of miracle.*

Alice: They were so happy because they didn't have cell service, they didn't have any money, and, you know, there was a store there, but no money. [*Laughs*]. What were they planning to do?

Richard: I was going to go into the store and beg, borrow, or steal. Or just beat 'em up and take the store away from them or something, use their phone.

Dean: It was one of those funny moments where only on an adventure like that do you get it, do you understand the humor in it. How was Mom in Butteville at the same time as we were? How did that happen? But finding her right when we needed to just seemed to wipe away the frustration of the day.

And it's moments like those on the Willamette that I will look back on later in life and treasure as some of the best.

"I will hold you,

hear you,

heal you.

Let me roll over your mind and wash through your heart.

Swim in my arms, child,

until your vision is clear."

~Mama River Whispers

EIGHT

Dean: When you set out to become the first person in history to do something, like swim an entire river, and when you're doing it with two active forms of cancer and you're raising money for the Leukemia and Lymphoma society along the way, you'd think the news stations would be all over that kind of story.

But they just weren't.

Not at first.

Lisa: I remember being at home when Dean first started swimming and emailing all the news stations. At first, they didn't do anything with it, so I was kind of disappointed.

Richard: The Corvallis newspaper came and interviewed him on the spot.

Dean: Corvallis/Albany is when we really started to get coverage, but, by that point we were almost 100 miles into this thing, about halfway done. I don't know if they thought it was too crazy, what I was doing, or not impressive enough. The closer we got to Portland, though, the more people started to become interested in what I was doing.

Alice: The Gresham radio station.

Richard: Channel 12.

Lisa: I remember emailing those news stations in Portland again because he'd been on the news in smaller cities already. I sent the links to those interviews and then anyone who was interested contacted Dean directly.

Dean: I did several radio interviews for one of the Pacific Northwest's most popular news/talk stations, OPB.

Richard: Those interviews were over the phone so all Alice and I got to hear was from one side, Dean's side, but I think it would have been a lot of fun to have heard the interviewer at the same time so we could understand the dialogue between them.

Alice: And then most of the time the interviews went on before we even left for the day, so sometimes we didn't even get to hear Dean's side of it until it aired.

Travis: I'll never forget Dean did an OPB interview with Geoff Norcross on NPR. Geoff was asking Dean all these questions and one was about logistical issues.

Dean said, "I just have to say, a couple of the people who really helped me out with any issues like that were Travis Williams and Kate Ross at Willamette Riverkeeper."

I just thought that was really cool for Dean to even mention us. You know, some people might have said, "I'm amazing and I'm working so hard and my passion is this," and not mention anyone else who might have helped them.

That's all fine.

But Dean is different. He provides the bigger picture and gives shoutouts to the folks who help him, and I think that is so cool.

Dean: The day after I had to stop early in Butteville we were going to try to make it to Canby, which would have been about ten or so miles downriver from the dock where we'd stopped, but Dad and I started talking about it and we decided, based on how tired I was, to only make it to Boone's Ferry in Wilsonville and then go on to Canby the next day. Split it up. Give me some rest. Keep it light and easy and the body moving.

As soon as I knew all I had to do was make it four miles to Boone's Ferry, everything in me relaxed. I found my pace again. I was swimming strong.

I learned later that one of the major news networks in Portland aired a story about me on TV the day before. Because of that press coverage, everyone we met on the river knew who we were. They'd call out to us from their docks or slow down in their boats. Dad was loving it. He'd paddle over and talk to them for a while, hand them one of my swimming in miracles bracelets.

That kind of thing—people recognizing us—continued day after day. But the coolest encounter happened the day we were swimming out of Wilsonville. There is a railway bridge that crosses the Willamette right before the I-5 bridge. I'd seen it many times from the freeway, but never really thought about it much until I was swimming up to it. There was a train slowly moving across it and I thought it would be so fun to go under the bridge while the train was crossing. Then, suddenly, the train stops right in the middle of the bridge. I didn't even know if it was legal for them to do that, and I was so shocked I stopped swimming. The engineer stuck his head out of the engine and started pulling on the whistle and yelling out our names.

Dad would never admit it, but I think it got him choked up. It was just so unexpected and so, I don't know, affirming? It was the first time I really knew I was probably going to finish this thing and that what I was doing was not stupid or thoughtless or uninspiring, but that I was actually having an effect on other people—people I'd never met. It felt like all of my hard work was paying off and what I was doing mattered to somebody other than just me.

Once we passed the railway bridge, the current started back up again, but with the return of the current came the return of civilization. More than we'd seen so far on the river. Both sides of the river were lined with nothing but big houses with massive, oftentimes elaborate, docks. We weren't used to so many people and so many houses and so many boats—fishing boats, motor boats—everywhere.

The river was still beautiful, but it very quickly went from wild and scenic to residential.

It felt congested.

It felt unnatural. Like lipstick on a pig. *[Laughs]*.

These docks and houses and boats all seemed too artificial for the river. In some ways, they took away the elegance and power of the river.

Dr. Watters: I flew out from Kansas for Dean's big fundraising gala toward the end of his swim.

Dean: When I arrived in Canby, Dr. Watters was there at the boat dock with Mom. When I got out of the water, he gasped. He said, "Shit, Dean. take off your wet suit."

And he started pinching me, and I'm like, "I miss you, too, Aaron."

Dr. Watters: I was checking his body fat.

Dean: "You're down below 3% body fat," he said. Dad walked up just as Aaron was saying, "Is there any possibility of taking tomorrow off?"

Dad's like, "Why?"

"I think Dean is seriously low on body fat."

This was a Friday and we had planned to swim Saturday morning and go to the Leukemia and Lymphoma Society's fundraising gala that night, but we decided just to take Saturday *and* Sunday off.

I slept most of the morning and afternoon on Saturday. I probably would have slept longer if I hadn't had the gala to go to.

I wasn't looking forward to it, if I'm being honest, because I was very disappointed by how little money we had raised.

When I first started thinking about raising money as I swam, I thought Portland would go crazy and we'd raise millions of dollars.

We ended up raising somewhere between $12,000 and $16,000. I can't remember the exact number.

However, a lot of the other teams who were raising money at the time came up to me at the gala and told me that a lot of their fundraising success was because I had been able to get the word out to so many people. So that made me feel good. Like I hadn't completely let the Leukemia and Lymphoma Society down.

After the weekend of the gala, I still had almost a full week left to go on my swim. Just because the fundraising was over, didn't mean my journey was.

Richard: When people first heard that Dean was gonna swim the river, one of the things they would ask was: "How is he going to swim over Willamette Falls?"

Dean: That's still everyone's first question.

"Did you swim through the falls?"

[Sighs, slightly annoyed]. I get so tired of that question, honestly.

Travis: Dean and Richard had people help them and give advice, but they were still the ones out there doing it. They were the ones who had to deal with the inherent dangers of the river.

Dean: Willamette Falls looks almost exactly like Niagara Falls only it's shorter and narrower. Instead of falling hundreds of feet, it only falls about eighty or ninety. I've learned since then that the falls is ranked second in the contiguous United States as far as water volume is concerned.

So, yes, it's going to be harmful to a swimmer, and the falls are nothing to be trifled with.

When people ask, I just try to keep it light so I'll joke and tell them I couldn't get a barrel sponsor so I portaged around.

Richard: We didn't try to maneuver that dangerous stretch of river. Didn't even want to get close to it. I mean, they have a system in place for boats—a lock system—but that's not made for swimmers. So we skipped from just above the falls to just below the falls to be safe.

Dean: After the falls, it wasn't long and we were creeping into the suburbs of Portland. Oregon City. West Linn. Gladstone.

Alice: Where did Mindy and her friend show up? Was that Milwaukie?

Richard: I believe so.

Alice: On the boards—oh, what do you call 'em?

Richard: Paddle boards.

Alice: Oh, yeah, paddle boards. And they went along with you for—

Richard: All day. The photographer Stephen Cridland was there then, too, taking pictures from his yacht.

Alice: Yeah.

Richard: In fact, I'm sure they all came through Lake Oswego with us because our financial advisor had an office on the river there and I told him we would be coming by and to watch out for us.

"Did you see me and Dean come through?" I asked him afterward.

"No," he said. "I kept looking out the window at the river, too. I saw a pretty good sized yacht. And two chicks on paddle boards."

"You crazy guy," I said. "If you had looked a little further ahead of them you would have seen us. Me in the kayak and Dean swimming."

He saw the two gals on the paddle boards and completely missed us. *[Chuckles]*.

Those girls were awesome. Standing up all the time paddling. Even through little currents or ripples or waves from boats. Not phased at all. Like they were glued to those boards. They went most of the day with us, paddling their boards, and, of course, Stephen Cridland, who had the yacht. He had gone up to Eugene to take pictures at the beginning and then would meet up with us every once in a while along the way. It was fun to have him along. Sort of a low-key guy, and he had his dog, his yacht, lots of cups of coffee.

Alice: Very friendly and part of the gang.

Richard: He was friends with Mindy.

Alice: One of the paddle boarders.

Richard: She grew up with Lisa.

Alice: She was Lisa's best friend in high school.

Stephen: It was fun when we got down into the Portland Metro area, because it seemed like a lot of people knew what was going on.

They were yelling down to Dean from the towers or were out on their decks cheering and applauding and whistling and stuff.

I thought that was pretty cool.

Bre: I remember the evening Dad swam into Portland well because, even though it was a Wednesday night, I'd finally talked my boss into letting me take off early from work and drive into the city to watch him swim in.

It took my boss a while to agree to that, even. She rarely gave time off. Thankfully, her husband, who also worked at the summer camp and was a real outdoorsman himself, had been following Dad's swim and helped plead my case.

He said to my boss, "It's not every day your dad *swims* the entire Willamette. Let her go and be a part of it."

And she did.

Alice: When we got to Portland, a lot of different people showed up at Tom McCall Park to watch Dean.

Lisa: My husband Steve and I were there.

Dean: Travis Williams.

Alice: Family friends who we'd known since Dean was a kid.

Dean: A lot of the women who worked for the Leukemia and Lymphoma Society.

Alice: And, of course, Stephen Cridland was there taking pictures.

Dean: The whole day was just incredible.

We started out where we had stopped the day before at Willamette Park, which is an urban park a few miles upriver from Portland on the west side of Ross Island. The river along that stretch is wide open and the current is really moving.

About halfway into that leg of the journey, this KGW news helicopter started following us. Followed us for about thirty minutes or so.

I tried my best just to swim normally, but I could hear the chopper blades whirring as this thing was hovering fifty or sixty feet above me and, every now and again I'd glance up and see their camera trained on me, so I wanted to make sure my strokes looked good.

And man, I'm stretching way out and just burning up the river, swimming like I'm some kind of Olympian.

Finally Dad said, "Hey buddy, you're swimming pretty fast. Slow down, because we promised the journalists and everyone else we would meet them downtown at seven o'clock sharp."

We wanted to make sure we timed it perfectly since we expected so many people to be downtown waiting, and after the helicopter followed us, we thought for sure there'd be tons of journalists and maybe even the mayor of Portland. So, I tried my best to slow down and keep a normal pace. But for as long as that helicopter was over us it was hard to.

Bre: As we waited downtown, we could see the helicopter in the distance, hovering over the river. We couldn't see Dad or Grandpa yet, but we were almost positive they were filming them. Then, they got a little closer and I could see Grandpa's kayak and the flashes of orange on the arms of Dad's wetsuit and we knew.

Lisa: It was awesome Dean could be recognized like that. I was so proud of him. *[Chokes up]*. Really proud of him.

Dean: After about thirty or forty minutes, the helicopter left, but so many people had seen it that they were sticking their heads out of their boat houses or jumping onto their decks, yelling our names and cheering us on.

Then, when we got closer, there was a dragon boat racing team on the river practicing. If you know nothing about the sport, it originated in China and the boats look like giant, elaborate canoes that hold about a dozen people who all paddle at once. It's very popular near Downtown Portland and when they get moving, they are fast. So, we saw this dragon boat, and they saw us and they came flying upriver toward us, shouting our names.

Richard: I said, "Dean, we've got to swim over there and talk to them."

Dean: They slowed down and, of course, Dad paddled over there. He was telling them all sorts of stories and laughing. After a while, he waved me over, wanted me to shake each of their hands.

Richard: Here's Dean, swimming from Eugene to the Columbia River, and they thought that was absolutely marvelous. We reached into the kayak and got all of them swimming in miracles bracelets, and you would have thought they'd just been given a medal in the Olympics. They were screaming at Dean. Thrilled.

Dean: But what happened next was about the coolest moment of my entire life.

When we set off from Willamette Park, it was a beautiful day—clear blue, fluffy white clouds—and by the time we encountered the dragon boat it had turned gray and was starting to sprinkle rain. Once we reached the Marquam Bridge there on the south end of downtown we still had about twenty minutes or so before we were supposed to swim into Tom McCall Park. So, we decided to hang out under the bridge for a little while and wait.

It had gotten a little foggy and, even though we were under this heavily trafficked bridge, the world seemed like it had gone totally quiet. Dad usually liked to fill the silence with talking, but there was something about that moment—being on Mama River, that otherworldly hush—that caused him not to. We just floated there in silence, looking out at Downtown Portland in the distance as it rose up out of the misty fog.

In that moment, I think it hit Dad and I both just how far we had come. The weeks and the miles and the moments we'd shared and endured.

For the first time since Mary died I was actually happy to be alive and, in my memory, that moment was almost like a reawakening, a rebirthing. It felt like all of the broken parts of me were finally starting to be glued back together. I got tears in my eyes, because it was just such a powerful moment and revelation that, even at the time, I remember thinking, *I will remember this moment for the rest of my life.*

Bre: The rain had really started to come down when Dad and Grandpa finally moved away from the Marquam Bridge and headed toward Tom McCall Park.

Dean: No one had an umbrella onshore.

Bre: It's Portland. No one uses an umbrella.

Dean: I think the rain kept the journalists away.

I had imagined swimming up and immediately being bombarded with microphones and a maelstrom of camera flashes, and I have to admit, I was a little disappointed when there was none of that. *[Laughs]*.

But then, very quickly, I was glad there wasn't a crowd of journalists.

It made the achievement of finally reaching Portland, just a handful of miles away from the Columbia, that much sweeter. Because it was only friends and family there. People who were really supporting me. People who knew me. Knew where I had come from. Knew how far I had gone already. Not just on the river, but in life. I don't want to use the word intimate, but that's exactly what it was. It was much more intimate and, I think, at that point, after my big revelation under the Marquam, it was exactly what I needed.

And then the unexpected happened.

Starting out from Eugene, first leg of the swim.

Aerial view of Dean captured by Stephen Cridland on Day 1.

Richard blazing through one set of rapids near Eugene.

Dean facing a thundering set of rapids.

Louis English, ready to roll.

Dean striding through the cool waters of the Willamette.

Richard, Alice, and Dean during a break.

Alice giving Richard a hand into the river.

Dean and sister, Lisa, at LLS Fundraising Gala.

Alice enjoying the epic Willamette adventure.

Bre and Dean being goofy before Dean's swim out of Salem.

Dean's uncle, David, studying a map of the river in Independence.

Dean's brother-in-law, Steve, niece, Kenzie, and Bre waiting for Dean and Richard to appear around the bend.

Richard and Dean slugging along in the river.

*"Cry into me.
Let me silence your screams.
Let me flow
with your fears."*

~Mama River Whispers

NINE

Alice: Once Dean got to Portland, there wasn't any doubt in my mind he wouldn't make it to the Columbia River.

Richard: The end was in sight. A hop, skip, and a jump and we would be there.

Dean: After we left City Center, the Willamette turned tidal, so we knew we had to time everything just right so I wasn't swimming against the current, but, even so, I thought the rest of the swim would be easy. Just two more days.

But I didn't account for the fact that Thursday, the day we left Portland, was June 26th.

Bre: June 26th was my mom's birthday. Dad and I each have our own struggles with those kinds of anniversary dates. My hardest day in terms of grief is always Mother's Day, because I really feel her loss that day, and Dad's toughest time is usually her birthday.

Dean: I woke up that morning all alone in the little duplex I was living in over in Gresham, and it was the first day of the swim I had woken up with Mary on my mind.

I think the swimming had distracted me from the overwhelming feeling of my grief for so long that the combination of it being her birthday and being the penultimate day on the river—seeing the end in sight—I was reminded that she wasn't around. That she wouldn't be there to see me accomplish my big dream.

And that feeling was miserable.

But I still had to get out of bed, put on my wetsuit, and get back into the river. I had almost eight miles to swim that day.

Travis: I paddled in my canoe with Dean from Downtown Portland onward. There was a power boat, another couple of paddlers, and Richard.

Dean: We all met back at the Portland Waterfront and, some dear family friends, Grace and Walt, who had watched me swim in the night before had enjoyed themselves so much, came back to see me off.

No one knew I was having a hard time emotionally that morning. I didn't tell anyone.

Grace and Walt knew Mary. They'd met her several times when we'd come back to Oregon to visit from Kansas. I don't know how it came up, but they all started recounting Mary stories. I did my best to talk, but it was very difficult to croak out even a few words. Then, rather than just have a quiet time of prayer the way we usually did, Walt led us in a time of prayer remembering Mary. I had the hardest time not breaking down and sobbing. Of course, the tears came anyway, but I tried to be discreet. I quickly picked up Dad's kayak and started moving into the water so no one could really notice.

Once I started swimming, it was just a relief to be moving and not feel stuck in my emotions.

I have to say, swimming through Downtown Portland was stunning.

Here were all the buildings I'd seen my entire life, all the bridges I'd grown up crossing, and yet they seemed different. It was a perspective I'd never before had of my hometown. I couldn't help but appreciate it, even though, internally, I was overwhelmed by my grief.

After we passed beneath the hulking, red Broadway Bridge—my favorite—on the north end of City Center, I was already tired because, with the tidal influence, there was no current to assist my strokes. I was just swimming through this slack water like I had in Newberg.

Then, it started raining.

Hard.

And everything I'd been feeling about Mary bubbled up and over. I started crying.

At first, I resisted. I think it was that old social belief taking over. The one that says real men don't cry, but then I thought, *if I'm gonna cry, it's the perfect day to do so. I'm already wet, it's raining, and if my goggles fill up with water nobody is gonna know.*

I don't think anyone *did* know. I don't think they could tell.

Richard: I could see the energy levels in Dean had come back in max and there was nothing—come hell or high water—going to stop him from making it to the Columbia.

Travis: Watching him swim that day, I couldn't help but think, *there it is. There's all this work and effort and he's just on the threshold of finishing.*

Dean: The stretch of river from the Portland bridges to Cathedral Park in St. Johns mirrored almost perfectly how I was feeling internally.

I thought the big houses with gorgeous yards and trees down around West Linn and Lake Oswego seemed unnatural, but it had nothing on the industrial area past Portland. Dilapidated docks. Burned-out warehouses. Slimy, rusted boats. It was all so depressing.

The further I swam, the more I cried, the more my goggles started to fog over from the tears. It seemed like there was no hope in that portion of the river. No hope within me. Just a terrible grief that felt like 500 pounds of weight had been put on my chest and like somebody had sucker punched me in the gut at the same time. There was this sick feeling in my stomach, too, like I was going to throw up—I feel that a little now just remembering it.

I used to think depression made a person feel heavy. Just dragging them down. I spent most of my 20s depressed.

But nothing feels as heavy as grief.

Bre: And no one really talks about the weight of grief or the specifics of how it feels. They don't talk about grief in general, it seems.

That perplexes me.

It's like, as a society, we've brought all of these other emotions into the light. Depression, anxiety. Take a pill, go to counseling, it's okay to feel that way, own it.

But grief hasn't been coaxed out as a "safe" emotion to feel outwardly. Not yet. Not in my opinion.

Grief is something most people think has a timestamp, too. A very short timestamp. Months. Maybe a year. And then you should be better. You should be fixed. You should not feel the grief any longer.

That's what some people think. It's what I've been told by family and friends on occasion, at least.

But, in the river, Dad chose to feel his grief, and I think that helped him more than he can ever explain.

Dean: I have never had as much of a relief from grief as I have had out in nature. That movement, that natural environment. It can definitely make you feel lighter.

I think the world needs to know that trees and rivers and oceans and lakes are here to partner with us. To help us heal. I wasn't just in the river floating, but taking an active part. You don't accidentally start swimming. You have to make that choice. There is power in that. Willpower. If I hadn't been on the water that day, I probably would have tried to numb myself by binge watching a TV series, trying my best to ignore my feelings and just get through the day rather than let them flow through me and find a way to honor Mary by honoring my broken heart.

Toward the end of that day, my grief started to alleviate and dispel. It was still kind of raining, but I remember seeing these bright raindrops catching the light of the sun that was trying to peek through the clouds. The rain would bounce off of the river and almost explode with light. It felt like the grief was being washed away and I was being cleansed by these tiny droplets of light. It was exhilarating.

Travis: We stopped at a couple of spots along the river for Dean to take a break.

"Hey, how are you feeling?" I asked once.

"Great," he said. "I'm tired, but the end is near, and I can see it, and it feels awesome."

Just the energy that day. You know, here's this guy who's about to finish swimming the Willamette, he's got just a few miles to go. That was cool to be a part of.

Richard: Our plan was to stop at Cathedral Park just on the other side of the St. Johns Bridge. Right before we reached the bridge, the tide started to turn. The current started to flow back into Portland and push us in the wrong direction.

Dean: I had to swim as hard as I possibly could to make it to the bridge. Just fighting the current like crazy to get past it. Thankfully, the park where we were stopping at was just on the north side of the bridge, so I didn't have too far to go, but, boy, did it take effort.

Dad always seemed so happy to have the day done and over with, but that day he was even more thrilled to be off of the water than usual. As I was walking up the boat ramp he was hugging and kissing Mom, laughing and talking to me and everyone else who was there. We had only one day left and everything was pointing to success.

I never told Dad what I'd been through emotionally that day. I don't think he ever knew. It was something I shared just between myself and Mama River. I've never talked about it, really. I've never told anybody the full story until now.

"You heard my call.

You dove in,

joined in my song.

You danced with me,

swam with me, and

now my waters will swim

in you

forever."

~Mama River Whispers

TEN

Alice: The last day, I was finally able to join Dean and Richard on the river.

Lisa's friend, Mindy, and Mindy's husband, Cory, brought their boat down to Cathedral Park, and a lot of us joined them to watch Dean swim.

I can't remember. Did we ride ahead of them? Or did we follow? I guess we were all over the place.

Richard: You just followed us, Alice. You'd go a little ways ahead, stop, and then we would come by.

Dean: Stephen Cridland had brought up his yacht and then Mindy and Cory had their boat. Mom was on it. Walt and Grace. And, of course, my sister Lisa wanted to be there for the big finish.

Lisa: We were waiting and watching and following them, taking pictures. The closer we got to the Columbia, the more excited we got.

Dean: Travis followed along in his big, green Old Town canoe with his daughter. He congratulated me on making it to the last day.

Travis: That very last day was a bit windy, if I recall. There were some showers coming, too. That area is just big, open water. An industrial stretch of river, you know. All the stuff along the shoreline with big boats moving along on one side while we were going down on river right.

It was a very different river than what Dean swam in back in Eugene.

Dean: That day was only gonna be a six mile swim. Every moment seemed to slow down, and I saw everything in high relief. Bright-blue, beautiful skies. These clouds that were dark underneath but had silver fringes. The light shining on the water was gorgeous, like gold. I felt as if it was Mama River saying, "Well done. You've done it."

Not yet, I thought.

Then I heard her again. "Yeah, but it's just gonna be a fun ride."

So, I got into the water and started to swim.

We had timed it really well with the tide, but it was odd because there were almost these two-foot rollers pushing me along. Almost like Mama River was patting me on the back and congratulating me. It made swimming super easy. I felt like I could swim all day long. As cliché as it sounds, it felt like I was dreaming, because it was everything I had visualized and hoped it would be and, yet, so much more.

But the closer I got to the finish, the more I didn't want it to end.

It felt bittersweet. It had been such a great adventure, and I felt like I'd been on the river for years instead of weeks. I couldn't even remember what my life away from the river was like or even what I had felt like before I started swimming, because everything I had experienced on the Willamette had changed me so much.

I just couldn't believe it was coming to an end.

Richard: Did I fall in love with the river the way Dean did? No.

Did I fall in love fall in love with the trees that bordered the river? No.

I don't think like him. I appreciate nature. I thank the Lord for it. But I'm not one that goes deep into my inner soul and comes out with all these really touchy things. I'm just sort of a rock. Yeah. An inanimate rock. And the rains come, the snows come, winter comes, then dry. And there I am.

I don't philosophize about my experiences. I am just sort of a basic guy. I'm not deep.

Doesn't mean I didn't enjoy our adventure any less. That journey? Just a thrill. Yeah, an absolute thrill.

Dean: Suddenly, we were in the wide-open mouth of the Willamette, staring out into the Columbia River. Compared to the Willamette, the Columbia is massive. Where is bisects the Willamette it's about a mile wide, flows swiftly, and is thwarted by heavy, heavy boat traffic. Not just small speedboats or fishing boats. We're talking massive barges hauling goods either toward Portland or toward Astoria, where the Columbia dumps into the Pacific Ocean.

I popped my head up out of the water and looked to Dad, thinking, *we're right here at the edge of the Willamette, are we finished?*

Dad said, "You need to go farther into the Columbia."

Richard: Dean was always worried about the stopping point of his swim. He wanted to make sure he really made it into the Columbia so that some butt head wouldn't come back and say, "Well, you really didn't get to the Columbia, you stopped Kelly Point Park and that's not really the Columbia River."

And Dean drilled it into my mind early on that we needed to make sure we got into the Columbia River. So that's what we did. We went beyond the mouth of the Willamette.

I paddled up to Cory's boat and told him, "I want you to take your yacht and stop in the Columbia River. We'll use you as our anchor point so that we know we've made it."

Dean: Stephen Cridland stayed closer to the mouth of the Willamette, taking pictures of Dad and me from a distance, but Mindy and Cory decided to throw down their anchor farther out so I could swim to their boat.

Richard: Well, Cory went out there in the *middle* of the Columbia River—

Alice: It wasn't really in the middle, but it was out quite a ways.

Richard: He dropped his anchor right in the middle of all that river traffic.

Alice: Right in the main channel. It's—

Richard: A boat highway pretty much.

Alice: None of us knew that it was, and I definitely don't think Cory knew.

Richard: I wasn't thinking that he'd actually drop his anchor, but he did. Anyway...

Dean: I started swimming again and Dad started paddling and suddenly we're moving into the main navigational channel of the Columbia, trying to get to our boat.

Richard: Here came this barge with a big—you might have seen them in the Columbia if you've spent time in the area— smiley face painted on it. It was coming toward us. You know, *vgssst [imitating horn]. Vgssst.*

Dean: We'd had a lot of boats, especially large boats the past day or so who would honk and wave at us.

Richard: Most of the barge guys were very friendly. *Tweet-tweet* on the horn and then stick their heads out and wave at us all friendly. So, we thought this barge was doing the same thing, but—

Alice: They were trying to tell us all to get out of the way. That they couldn't stop.

Stephen: I know some of those guys who run the barges, and I know they don't have any patience for tomfoolery from recreation boats.

Dean: Stephen, who was still a bit upstream and out of the main channel, got on his PA and shouted at us. "Guys, they're not saying hello. They're fully-loaded. It would take them over a mile to stop. You're going to get run over."

Richard: We were dead-on in the way of this thing.

Dean: Cory started trying to get his anchor up, but it got stuck on something so they couldn't get over to us. And this giant barge with a happy face painted on it was still barreling toward us.

Then Stephen Cridland shouted again, "Swim, Dean, swim."

Richard: That's when I knew we were in trouble.

Lisa: I was on Mindy and Cory's boat, looking at my brother and father, who were full-on in the way of this massive ship. They looked so tiny compared to it that I literally thought to myself, *They are going to get swallowed up.*

Richard: I looked down and told Dean, "Swim. Swim hard."
He started to swim like crazy.

Dean: Dad swung his kayak around in one, quick swoop and took off back toward the Willamette. He shouted over his shoulder, "Follow me."

I jumped behind him and swam for all I was worth.

Richard: I turned my boat around. I had the wind with me and the waves, so I was zipping over there to the shore.

Dean: Luckily, I swam hard enough and got out of the way. The barge was about thirty yards away from me when it passed, but when the news casters, who were on the shore filming all of this, made it look like it barely missed me.

Richard: After the barge went by I thought, *I know Dean survived, but I don't know where Stephen is or Cory—where's Cory?*

Then I saw his boat, and he was out of the danger zone, too.

Dean: Honestly, I didn't feel like I was in any danger until the barge passed. I was still waving at him like I was in a parade and, once I realized not only was he not congratulating me or happy with me, but was actually yelling obscenities, the reality of how horribly wrong it could have all gone sank in, and I felt lucky we made it out of the way.

Richard: I was very happy everybody came out alive on that one.

Dean: Soon, it was time to get onto the boat and step out of the water for the last time. Whatever panic or confusion or relief I felt about not being run over by the barge quickly dissolved, and in its place was immense happiness.

I had finally achieved my big dream.

Not only that, but I felt healthier and stronger than I did when I began.

Richard: Dean got onto Stephen's boat, and he was doing all sorts of antics, showing off.

Alice: Making the figure head at the front of the boat.

Dean: I did my best *What About Bob* impression.

Lisa: "I'm a sailor. I sail."

Dean: "Ahoy!"

Richard: Then, we motorized back up the river to St. Johns. That's when a whole bunch of people joined us and we had a celebration on the docks.

Dean: As soon as we got back to Cathedral Park a news team—I can't remember which one. KOIN, I think. Anyway, they had a crew there to interview me and that felt like a fitting end. To have it documented by them. I remember blurting out, "Chasing your dreams has the power to create miracles...even bring you back to life." I had no idea how prophetic those words were at the time.

Once the interview was over, the rest of us stood around laughing and patting each other on the back and, of course, Dad had to take over and say a few words and a quick prayer. Then, rather than pop champagne, we popped sparkling soda. Poured them into plastic champagne glasses. It was fun. I don't think any of us could believe it was really over. It felt a little surreal at the time.

Richard: It was that night or the next night we had the dinner down at the—

Alice: Yeah, I remember that, but I can't remember which night. If it was the same day he finished. I don't think it was the same.

Richard: No, I think it was the next night we went to the Old Spaghetti Factory right on the Willamette, close to City Center. Had a big dinner to celebrate the whole shebang.

Alice: It was *really* something.

Richard: It was quite a journey. *[Shakes head in disbelief]*. Dean accomplished something most people would say they couldn't even attempt.

Bre: I couldn't get time off of work to be there that last day, but it didn't change the fact that I was so proud of Dad and what he had achieved. To this day, I am still so proud of what he accomplished on the Willamette, and I wish I'd had the guts to blow off work and watch him swim those final miles. I'd like to think I've made up for it since, taking over Grandpa's role and guiding Dad down two other rivers, the River Shannon in Ireland and the Eel in California.

But those are stories for another day.

Dean: It felt wonderful to finally be finished. A dream come true. One of the most satisfying things. I remember leaving Cathedral Park and feeling almost like I was walking on air. Everything looked brighter and more alive and I felt super strong.

But then I went home to the little duplex where I was living by myself. Within a couple of hours everything started to dim and fade.

I'd just accomplished something so big in my mind and had been going after this dream for months in a way that was all-consuming and then, suddenly, it was over. There was nothing left for my mind to consume. Nothing left for my heart to concentrate on.

I didn't know what to do.

PART III

"You swam to live,
now live to swim.
You moved with me,
now let me move you.
You felt my flow,
now flow with all of Creation's mystery and majesty.
As long as you have life—
move, breathe, bend,
live."

~Mama River Whispers

ELEVEN

Dean: For several days following the swim, all I did was sleep. I was so exhausted emotionally and physically, that's all I could do, really.

Then I heard the family was all going down to Mom and Dad's beach house for July 4th, so I decided to go along. We had a nice time, and once everyone left, I stayed down for a week or so afterward on my own.

That's when I really started to feel lost.

I lapsed back into heavy, heavy grief, and I just didn't know what to do. I spent a lot of time at the beach, sitting on the sand dunes, watching the ocean, praying and asking, *what's next?*

It was then I realized two things. First, I felt very strongly that the next step in life was to find another river to swim, but this time do whatever I could to make sure Bre was a part of the journey. I felt like she needed time on the river the way I did.

Bre: Actually, Dad pitched the idea of the two of us hot air ballooning across the United States together first. I'm terrified of flying and heights, but he hooked me with the line: "It would make for an epic adventure you could write about."

Thankfully, that dream died within a few months and river swimming was back at the forefront of his mind.

Dean: The second realization I had on the beach stemmed from the fear that I might get really sick again, and I just felt God or life or the universe—whatever you wanna call that beautiful force—impress upon me: *Nope, you've suffered enough. All you have to do now is continue to adventure and tell your story and inspire others.*

So, that gave me hope again, and I started researching other rivers I could swim.

Around that same time, Mom and Dad were pushing me to go to the doctor and get a blood test to see how my cancer was doing.

I felt really strong physically, but what scared me was my lymph nodes kept growing and growing. It wasn't until January or February of 2015 that I went to OHSU in Portland to get a biopsy done. There, I was formally diagnosed with small cell non-Hodgkin's lymphoma.

Because of that diagnosis, I assumed my leukemia was doing poorly again, too, so I flew down to San Diego in March of that year to see the specialist I'd been to the year before. He took samples of my blood and when he came into the room to deliver the results he looked shocked.

He said, "If I hadn't diagnosed you myself I would have said you never had leukemia in the first place. I've been doing this for over thirty years and I've never seen this happen. I cannot officially diagnose you with leukemia anymore."

Once you have the type of leukemia I had—Chronic Lymphocytic Leukemia—you're supposed to always have it. You're not supposed to ever be able to get rid of it.

I asked the specialist, "Why do you think it's gone?"

"My best guess," he said, "is your swim. Constantly moving the body, constantly boosting your immune system, constantly being in that cold, cold water. These are all theories, of course, but that would be my best guess."

Richard: I had never thought the river would heal his cancer.

Alice: Not ahead of time, no.

Richard: It was one thing for a guy who had leukemia and lymphoma to get into a river and swim the entire thing, but it was something else to see that cold water and that exercise help him the way it did. The Lord absolutely performed a miracle there.

Dr. Watters: There is nothing in the medical literature that suggests getting into a river, or out in nature for extended periods, makes people better. However, I watched it. I watched it happen.

Dean: I was stunned by what the specialist had said. That he thought my time in the river had eliminated the leukemia.

"But your lymphoma is not doing well at all," he said. "We're going to check it again in a couple of months, and if it's not improving, I'm going to suggest you do a round of chemo."

"You know how I feel about that," I said.

"Yes," he said. "But it's getting really bad, Dean."

That's when I thought, *if the river helped my leukemia, then there has to be something to help my lymphoma. Something in nature.*

I had heard of a practice in Japan called shinrin-yoku, or forest bathing, and Nippon Sport Science University in Tokyo did several research studies showing that spending just a few hours in the forest will boost the immune system and cancer-fighting cells for up to three weeks after, if I'm remembering correctly.

In my mind, I thought if I started going out to the forest, to the Mt. Hood Wilderness area—which was only a forty-five minute drive from my house—once per week, it would start a snowball effect.

So, I started going to the forest every Thursday night and staying through Friday afternoon, usually. If I hadn't already swum the Willamette and seen results from that, then I might not have had the courage to gamble my life like that again. But I thought to myself, *if the river healed me and I didn't know it had that ability, then it wasn't the placebo effect, so there has to be some merit in this theory. There must be something to the idea of nature as healer.*

Travis: There's a lot to the idea of nature as healer, I think. Whether it's psychological, whether it's physical—I think anytime you're able to get outdoors generally, being able to get off of the phone and electronics and enjoy what's right there in front of you and to be in that moment. I think that "being in the moment" aspect was something Dean was experiencing all the time on the Willamette. All of his thoughts were related to swimming. I think something can be said for that.

But I think anything related to being outdoors and moving the body to some degree is inherently healthy.

Louis: I'm a big believer in nature as healer.

Al: I don't know what effect being in nature would have on someone's physical health, but I know it has a huge effect on the mental health of a person. And that's been proven.

Dean: After a year of going out into the forest once per week, my lymph nodes had shrunk back to a normal size and, by March of 2016, the lymphoma was gone.

I was completely cancer free.

Louis: It was just phenomenal what happened to the cancer after Dean's swim.

Al: Pretty spectacular.

Louis: I think Dean having cancer actually helped him swim the Willamette, because, in his mind, he had nothing to lose.

Dr. Watters: Those alternative methods worked for Dean, and I'd like to think they could work for other people, too, but I don't think most people have the willpower to complete that kind of a task.

Thomas P. Seager, PhD (*Co-founder Morozko Forge; Associate professor, Arizona State University*): When you're facing a terminal diagnosis, it gives you a certain kind of freedom. A freedom that most people will never have the courage to take advantage of.

When I first heard about Dean and what had happened with his cancer as a result of swimming the Willamette, I didn't believe his story could be generalized to other people. I wasn't questioning his experience per say, but here I'm coming from this academic background and I'm a scientist and I'm thinking, *show me the data.*

Dean had this undeniable experience.

But the experience of one individual does not create a hypothesis that extends to other people. I thought it was only unique to Dean.

Dean: I started taking ice baths while I was training for my swim simply to prepare my body for the Willamette, since it is largely a snowmelt river. I expected the cold to shock me at first. I anticipated that after-drop post-ice bath. What I didn't expect was the effect those ice baths would have on my grief. One of the first things I noticed, in fact, was that after a couple of minutes in the cold bath, that 500 pounds I always felt on my chest wasn't there. The grief had been alleviated by the cold. With everything I knew as a therapist, it made no sense how I would be able to get immediate relief from my grief.

I knew cold water had the ability to aid me physically as well as emotionally, so, even after the swim, I became deeply committed to doing ice baths daily. That meant I was spending around eighty to one-hundred bucks on bags of ice every day and schlepping them from the grocery store to my house.

Finally, I decided there had to be a better way. I just needed to look for it. That's when I got online and found Tom and Morozko Forge.

Thomas: Jason, my former student and now my business partner, and I were doing the same thing as Dean: hauling ice. But we live in Phoenix, Arizona, and the damned thing about living here during the summer is, if you want an ice bath, you gotta start with at least two-hundred pounds of ice. We would go over to Jason's back yard, which was about 110-degrees in the summer, and fill up an old stock tank with ice. I'd get in for five minutes, Jason would get in for five minutes, and, if anyone else was with us, it was almost forty-five-degrees in that tank before the last guy could even get in.

We thought, *you know this is better than nothing, but it's also kind of ridiculous. We're both engineers. Can't we figure out how to make our own ice?*

I did my doctoral dissertation on environmental thermodynamics, but the fact is that the idea of making ice in the middle of the desert seems like a miracle.

It took us weeks of pulling apart freezers and building ugly prototypes, but we managed to figure out the engineering of it, and we made ice.

To understand what the forge looks like, imagine a stock tank—very low tech. We've built a wooden box around it and insulated it and run refrigeration coils underneath it. It has a compressor, and it makes ice.

The forge was the first cold plunge that could make its own ice. Now it's not the only one out there, but it was the first.

Dean: When I found Morozko Forge online and saw their ice baths, I thought, *why not throw a Hail Mary pass and share my story and tell them I could be their senior citizen poster boy if they sent me a forge for free.*

And they actually didn't ignore me or laugh at me.

Thomas: Well, we've done a lot of laughing together since then.

Dean: *[Laughs]*. Yes.

But at first they actually took me seriously.

Not only did we start some wonderful conversations, but they sponsored me with the forge that I'm still using daily.

Thomas: Dean's experience with cold water and his cancer story was very appealing, but, honestly, one of the reasons we said yes to sending him a forge was, at the time, we had never shipped one farther than California, and we had done that with our own equipment, our own van. We had never used a freight shipper.

We thought, he's not gonna be mad at us if it gets banged up or doesn't make the trip from Arizona to Oregon. He's gonna be patient with us. Right? Because we're sponsoring him. We're giving him a forge in exchange for promotion and storytelling and stuff like that, so let's give it a shot.

That was our first experiment. Trying to figure out whether we could sell and deliver a forge that we weren't delivering ourselves. Dean seemed like the right guy to be our test customer.

And it seemed to work really well.

Dean: I instantly fell in love with the forge. I loved that it made its own ice. I loved that it stayed cold even if I turned if off for a few days. I loved the rough-cut look of it, too. It gave me some outdoor, manliness I desperately needed in suburbia.

Thomas: Dean was super enthusiastic when he got the forge, and I'm like, *we gotta get to know him better.*

Dean: We did some video calls and a podcast and really started to connect.

Thomas: Then something happened to me along the way.

I was getting my blood work done. I'm checking all the boxes—give me this panel and that. One of them is the men's health panel and you get your testosterone checked. *Rrggh. [Flexes muscles].* I wanna know that, you know? Along with that, you get the prostate specific antigen, and I didn't even know what that was until it came back on my lab report with a red exclamation mark, because mine was 7.8, and at my age, anything above a 4 is an elevated risk for cancer.

That scared the crap out of me.

Even though the PSA is not the most reliable test, I did not wanna go back into the medical system and start getting the physicals and the biopsies without talking with people, without educating myself.

So, I started talking with guys about prostate health. It turns out that men don't talk anywhere near enough about these kinds of things with one another. They don't share their stories. It's not like we say, let's go get a beer and talk about our prostates. It's just not the kind of conversation that we're used to having. But, after the stories I got from older men and some younger men, I realized I didn't want anything to do with surgeries or biopsies. I decided I would rather die a long, slow, miserable death—that was the story I was telling myself, at least—from prostate cancer than go through the established medical procedures.

And, of course, Dean was on my mind.

So, you know, I'm a scientist, right? What do I do? I go to the library and try and see how it is that Dean cured himself.

Dean: I didn't know that when I got into the river up in Eugene I would be cured of my leukemia by the time I reached the mouth of the Willamette outside of Portland. I had no idea. I just didn't wanna die on a couch, so I was just trying to swing for the fence and do one last thing before I died.

But that cold water. That movement.

It did something miraculous.

A lot of people, especially folks who follow Wim Hoff and other cold water immersion experts, have told me, "Well, it must have been the placebo effect."

It couldn't have possibly been the placebo effect.

Thomas: A placebo effect requires the subject to have a psychological expectation of benefit. If the subject is unaware of the placebo, then it's not the placebo effect, because it is the story that the subject is telling themselves that creates this powerful placebo effect.

I'm getting this from Dr. Bruce Lipton. He wrote a book called *The Biology of Belief*. Basically, all of the cells in your body have no choice but to respond to the signals that they're getting from the brain. That's biochemistry. Nerves, hormones. The cells are signaled, and they respond.

The placebo effect requires your brain to have an experience that tells a story that generates a biochemical response to which the cells must respond.

And there's nothing wrong with that. I love the placebo effect. It's the one effective treatment that doesn't have deleterious side effects, you know? What's better than a placebo for goodness sake?

But nobody told Dean, "Get in the water. Swim around a little bit. Your blood's gonna be fine."

Dean: As a matter of fact, they told me the opposite.

Thomas: This is the way I run my life sometimes. I look at the people I admire and I choose them as role models.

I say, "I want some of what he's got. I want some of what he's got. I want—"

It's not that I wanna become that person, but the things that I admire about their life I wanna bring into my own life.

Dean brought this miraculous health approach into his life that I wanted for myself.

So, after my blood test results, I started reading. The best resource I found was Travis Christofferson's *Tripping over the Truth*. In it, he talks about the Warburg Effect and how the science of cancer has been set on the wrong course by all the money that is underlying it. The book talks about Nixon, who founded what he called the "War on Cancer". I'm so sick of war metaphors. This was in the middle of the Vietnam War, and people are protesting the Vietnam War, and Johnson had a war on poverty, and Nixon's like, "Okay, well we're gonna have another war!"

Like all those other wars, there were people—war profiteers—who were profiting from them, and government spending is actually meant to perpetuate the war rather than resolve it.

That summarizes fifty years of National Cancer Institute approaches to cancer treatment. They see it as a genetic mutation disorder. They see it as something requiring super-high technology.

Now, you can't quote me on the exact figure, but the Warburg Effect points out that approximately 80% of cancer cells can only metabolize glucose. It makes sense, because glucose is water soluble, unlike fat and lipids, and it is such a densely-packed energy that it is the best fuel for cancer cells, and many cancer cells can't survive without glucose.

Warburg hypothesized that if you starve the cancer cells of glucose, they will not grow, tumors will shrink, and they will collapse upon themselves from starvation.

If the body is not burning glucose because you've gone low carb then what is it burning? Ketones.

Christofferson followed up *Tripping over the Truth* with another great book called *Ketones, the Fourth Fuel*. So what are the fuels? Carbs and fats. That's two. In a pinch, your body can metabolize protein. That's three. What's the fourth? Ketones.

The book talked a lot about exogenous ketones. You can eat ketones and introduce them into your bloodstream through your diet, but the body will produce ketones as fuel for the cells, so these are endogenous ketones. Now, that book came out later, after my prostate scare, but what I learned from *Tripping Over the Truth* at the time was that cancer cells, almost all of them, require glucose. In the lab they exposed cancer cells to ketones and discovered that ketones kill cancer cells.

So, when you put yourself into ketosis there are two things that happen. One, you starve the cancer and two, you kill the cancer. Ketones are the body's natural chemotherapy.

I'm not knocking the concept of chemotherapy when I say ketones are the body's natural chemotherapy, but the beautiful thing about ketones is they feed your brain, kill your cancer, and have evolved over millions of years to become the perfect chemotherapy for the body. We can't do better than what nature has already endowed us with.

I don't know if I had cancer. I never even went for a prostate exam. I just saw the results of my blood test and said, "I'm gonna experiment with a ketogenic diet and cold exposure."

I knew when Dean was doing his cold water swimming going down the Willamette River, even in his wet suit, he was producing his own endogenous ketones. In that endurance environment, his body was burning through any of the carbs he ate and the only way his body could sustain itself in the cold water for hours at a time was on a ketogenic metabolism.

Dean: I had never even heard of a ketogenic diet at that time.

Thomas: But it explains how Dean drove his leukemia into—I don't even know what the right word is, 'cause remission doesn't seem like a strong enough word. Cure his leukemia? I'm not a medical doctor, so I don't know if that's the right word. Maybe remove. He removed all traces of leukemia from his body.

After my initial blood test, I thought, *I want that.*

I didn't achieve that by swimming, but with a ketogenic, low-carb diet, intermittent fasting, and cold exposure in the water.

Then I took another test. My PSA had gone from 7.2 down to 0.8, which is a super clean bill of health.

Bre: For years now, I've heard stories about the benefits of cold water. Dad's story. Tom's story. Tons of other people who have been able to reverse diagnoses or find relief. It still amazes me. I always think, *how incredible is that? I want to try it out.*

Richard: For a few months a year or so ago, Dean talked me into going to the Clackamas River every day. I'd get in for about half an hour up to my chest. It helped me sleep. Helped my emotional state. When I couldn't go to the river, I'd fill up the bathtub at home.

Louis: I've been taking cold showers since 2010. Ever since, I've read more about cold water swims and the immune system, and I think it can be very healing.

Bre: In the middle of putting this book together, both of my mom's parents passed away within months of each other. I had really done some work on my grief surrounding my mom's death in the years following Dad's Willamette swim, but the loss of my grandparents brought up a lot of old feelings and a lot of new ones I wasn't expecting. Just getting into a cold bathtub with a little bit of ice in my apartment for ten minutes or so every day helped me cope. And if I was having a tougher time than usual, I'd call Dad just to talk about it. His advice was always, "Get into some cold water and call me back if you don't feel better."

I always felt better.

Thomas: The first fifteen seconds before I get into the forge are always the hardest. Then, I get in, I'll experience the gasp reflex, which is a reflex meant to protect us, and then I'll settle right in and the anxiety will melt away.

Sometimes, you know, if I've had a fight with Amanda, I'll start shivering almost right away. If I'm angry at the world or there's something I need to process emotionally I start to shiver immediately. What is that? I've got plenty of brown fat, so I don't *need* to shiver anymore.

Peter Levine says to let the tremble happen because it's part of the body's response to trauma. So, I realize now, when I begin to shiver, I'm not shivering, I'm trembling. All of that anxiety, all of that trauma, is coming up to the surface.

Bre: I understand that concept of trembling vs. shivering completely, because whenever I've gotten into a cold bath while I'm still feeling intense emotions of grief, I shiver and shake right from the start. So, yeah. I get that concept. It really resonates with me and explains how cold water is working with me in those times.

Thomas: What is the most traumatic experience?

The birth experience.

It is the primal trauma of leaving the womb and coming into the world that starts our lives in trauma.

I'm putting all of this together in an incredibly speculative way. I'm saying Dean's people, Bre's people, my people, wherever they came from…and it was something before

Ireland—it was East Africa. They were all born into cold water.

Even if we don't like to swim, we experience the water—we experience the beach, the river, flotation tanks—as healing. Why is the water so healing? Because there is something about it that takes us back to the trauma of our birth, that envelops us in the environment for which our evolutionary biology says, "You are home. You are safe. You are cared for. You are where you belong."

When I first get in, I hold my breath instinctively, because that's the way I'm programmed, from before I was born—a baby will instinctively hold its breath underwater—and once I realize I'm okay and that this is what cold feels like and I take control of my breathing, I'm being reborn.

Dean: People have asked me since the swim, "Dean, how did you get in the river day after day after day?"

It depends on the person interviewing me, but my most honest response is: "I longed for it. I looked forward to getting back in the river, because, within minutes, I felt at home. I felt comfortable. I felt like I was back in my own skin. I felt alive."

I call the Willamette Mama River now, because it felt as if the water had taken on a persona. Like she was hugging me and comforting me after everything I'd been through the four years previous. So it wasn't hard for me to get back in the river every day, because it literally felt like I was back with Mama.

Thomas: That is such a touching metaphor. Mama River.

Travis: Dean's story is so encouraging. It inspires people in so many ways, but really, it inspires them to get outside. Find solitude. See wildlife. Do something physical. Whether it's swimming or paddling or hiking on the shoreline, I hope more and more people find the water. I think making a connection to water, whether it's the Willamette or another body of water, is very important.

Al: This is a great place in the world for people who like to paddle, because you don't have to go too far. And there's that saying, "You can only step in the same river one time". The river is always changing.

Louis: It's always flowing and your scenery is always changing. You can surf in the waves, you can practice you "gratuitous rolls" *[laughs]* if you want.
    It's all right there.
    And for the nominal price of a kayak, a paddle, and a jacket, it's endless entertainment.
    Or you can go lighter and just have a wetsuit and go swimming like Dean.

Alice: Dean's swim was so big, and for him to do it successfully just gave him a huge boost of confidence, and, of course, the cold water, I think, brought healing. Probably more than just physical healing, too.

Richard: It was absolutely incredible the way that Dean took those tough emotional and physical experiences that he'd been through and channeled everything into swimming the Willamette. Every muscle and tendon and bone in his body went into this thing. And, as he swam, he basically swam through all of the muck that was inside himself and swam into a freedom situation.

At the end of it, that was a weight off of his chest, his back, his shoulders. That weight was gone. That's what I was the happiest about.

Dean: I didn't know my cancer would vanish by me pursing my dream to become the first person in history to swim the entire length of the Willamette River. I didn't even *think* it might help me in that way. I was just trying to live while I had the chance.

As cliché as it sounds, we're not promised another day, we're not even promised another minute. Most of us walk through life thinking that someday we're going to be happy or someday our dreams will come true or someday we will be able to live life the way we want to, but the sad thing is, by the time "someday" comes around, most people are already dead.

When you reach the end of your life, what will you have done that you're the proudest of? What stories will you tell your grandchildren? Will they be about how much money you made working in some office or will they be about some great adventure you had while following a dream?

Life is the ultimate grand adventure. It's a thrill and it's a risk. It's incredible and it's terrifying. Things are gonna go awry. They're going to be hard. But if life wasn't a struggle, if it wasn't a torment, then there's no way it could also be an adventure. I think a lot of people believe courage is the absence of fear, but true courage is the ability to persist and proceed in the very presence of fear. That's where the growth is. That's where we have the power to become something greater and give meaning to our lives.

And that helps us answer the biggest question of all. The one we must ask ourselves again and again.

What does it mean to truly be alive?

AFTERWORD

Accomplishing my dream of becoming the first person to swim the entire length of the Willamette River changed everything for me. Of course, that doesn't mean my life was suddenly perfect.

I was no longer dying of cancer. I was no longer drowning in heavy, heavy grief after the loss of my first wife, Mary. But I still had to face a big question I hadn't yet dared to ask: What was I going to do with the rest of my life?

My therapy practice was almost nonexistent right after the swim. My daughter, Bre, was still weighed down by overwhelming grief from the loss of her mom. Not to mention, when the cheers and media excitement from my Willamette swim subsided, I began to feel extremely isolated and lonely.

However, the lessons I learned from the river and the steps I'd taken to accomplish my dream, gave me the tools to help me rebuild my life.

Within a year after the swim, I was working full-time again as a therapist and I had met and fallen in love with Bobbi, a personal trainer/fitness model who is as beautiful on the inside as she is on the outside. By the time Bobbi and I got married in December of 2016, I was already planning my next river adventure.

Ever since I had finished my Willamette swim, I had longed to put my daughter, Bre, on a similar healing path to help with her grief. So, I nagged her relentlessly (she's an adventurer at heart, so it wasn't a horrific nagging) until she finally relented to join me as my kayaker in my pursuit to become the first person to swim the entire length of the River Shannon in Ireland, while raising money and awareness for the Childhood Cancer Foundation of Ireland during the summer of 2017.

That swim was a success, and Bre will be the first to tell you that her time on the river was the beginning of her own healing journey.

Once I returned to the U.S., I started using the lessons I'd learned from my river adventures to help my clients heal from their trauma and anxiety in new and exciting ways. I believe, since modern talk therapy and coaching has been an indoor, intellectual pursuit for so long, there is only so much healing that can be done. But, by facing fears and healing wounds in the fresh air, braving the elements and allowing the wilderness to soothe traumas the same way it did for me, I believe the possibilities are endless.

For the past five years, I've been working on a passion project called "The Wild Cure Way". This new form of coaching encourages clients to get off the couch and do more than just talk about their problems. In the near future, it is my hope to lead groups and individuals on retreats in the wilderness, where they can discover the same ideals and modalities that were borne out of my own healing journey with rivers and forests.

When I look at where I'm at in life now—swimming in wild waterways around the world, writing about my journey and the practices that have healed me, teaching as many as I can how to accomplish their own impossible dreams—I know it is not a life my first wife Mary would recognize. I am sure, however, it would still make her smile, because she always saw the teacher, coach, and wild explorer inside of me.

Dean Hall

Dean's unique perspective of the Willamette—face-down.

Richard and Alice riverside before the day's journey.

Dean, Richard, Lisa, Bre, and Alice praying for safety before one leg of the swim.

Making it to St. Johns on June 26th.

Celebrating finally reaching the Columbia River and becoming the first person to swim the entirety of the Willamette.

Brock, Dean's nephew, dropping by the river to cheer his uncle on.

Dean doing his best *What About Bob* impression on the front of Stephen Cridland's boat to commemorate his achievement.

Dean forest bathing in the Mt. Hood National Forest post-swim.

Dean and wife, Bobbi, married in 2016.

Dean and Thomas P. Seager at a cold water event in Hood River, OR, 2021.

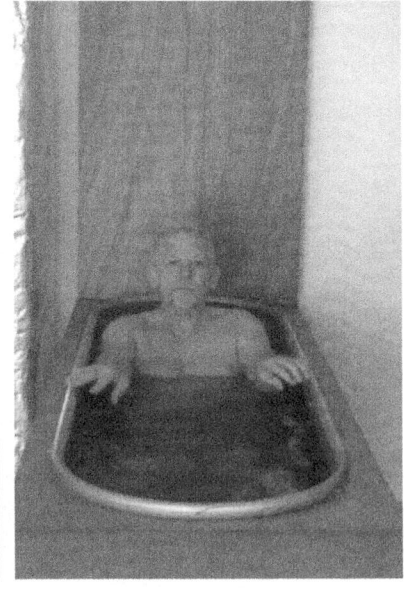

Dean using his Morozko Forge ice bath in 2019.

The adventure continues—Dean and Bre on the River Shannon, 2017.

Bre and Dean scouting a potential river swim, 2022.

Back: Matthew (Dean's nephew), Bre, Brock (Dean's Nephew).
Front: Bobbi, Dean, Alice, and Richard. Fundraising for Beads of Courage, 2022.

ACKNOWLEDGEMENTS

There are so many amazing people to thank for not only making this book possible, but the swim itself.

Travis Williams. Without your guidance and support, the swim might not have ever happened. You were the sign that Richard and Alice had asked for as an acknowledgement from God that this was an adventure they needed to support. For this, the first of many miracles, we can only say, thank you. Thanks, also, to **Kate** and the rest of the **Willamette Riverkeeper** for your support during the swim.

Dr. Aaron Watters. You have seen us both through some tough times in life, and, as always, we appreciate your generosity, love, and support.

Al Grapel and Louis English. The river legends! Thank you to the ends of the earth for the parts you played during the swim. You took a 79-year-old who had never kayaked and a 54-year-old who had an impossible dream and made it not only possible, but fun. Thank you, also, for sharing your own stories/wisdom of the river and allowing them to be included in this book.

Stephen Cridland. Thank you for the incredible photographs you took and the support you gave Dean on the river, as well as your participation in this book.

Thomas P. Seager. Thank you for your friendship over the years and your constant encouragement. We are especially grateful for the insights you contributed to the final chapter of this book as well as the wonderful foreword. A big shoutout to the rest of the **Morozko Forge** team, especially **Jason, Adrienne, and Amanda.** You are all rockstars and have affected both of us in more ways than you may ever know.

Lisa and Steve Tyler. Endless thanks for being a part of the book and the swim. And, of course, thank you for the years of love and support you have shown both of us. We love you so much!

Richard and Alice Hall. A special thanks to the two of you, who were not only there for every leg of the adventure itself, but sat through countless rounds of interviews to get these stories onto the page.

You are the OG adventurers of the family (you won't know exactly what that means, but when Bre explains it to you, you'll probably smile and/or feign embarrassment.).

Without your thirst for the outdoors and your willingness to share your love of nature with your children and grandchildren, our lives would have turned out very differently. You two mean more to us than words can say. We love you. Thank you, thank you, thank you.

A HUGE thank you to the incredible **Bobbi Parker Hall**, who has changed both of our lives for the better.

To Bobbi, from Bre: thank you for being the best stepmom anyone could ask for. Thank you for all of our amazing conversations and your endless support of me. I've always said no one could fill my mom's shoes, but dear Bobbi, you have found a way to put your own pair of shoes right next to hers. I know my mom would be grateful for that—because I am. Beyond grateful. I love you.

To Bobbi, from Dean: Thank you for showing me every day that pursuing impossible dreams, in life and in love, is not only a courageous choice, but the most practical. Catching you will always be a greater accomplishment than any and every world-record swim or fantastic adventure. Your love makes me believe that even my worst days were worth it since they led me to you. Your life and daily example inspires me to try harder, live bigger, and dare to dream of future impossible adventures even though we are at an age most would dream of nothing more than a comfortable rocking chair.

Thank you to everyone else who contributed to the swim itself, whether it was with boat support, morale support, or financial support—thanks a million!

Thanks to the rest of our friends and family who supported us on and off the page/river. We'd be here for another year if we listed you all, but you know who you are and what you did for us. We are forever grateful for your love, support, and general presence in our lives.

Finally, the ultimate thank you goes to Bre. Thank you for being such an incredible daughter who, since the day you were born, has been my greatest source of love, light, and laughter. You are the reason I fought to live full-volume when all I really wanted to do was die quietly. You are the one who gave me to the motivation to reach for something no one in history had ever accomplished at a time I believed my story was over. When I couldn't and wouldn't do it for myself, you inspired me to do it for you. And, now, you are the one who brought my story to life to share with others. Thank you for being a daughter who loves fully, a friend who gives freely, and a writer who tells stories fantastically.

Sorry, Dad, but the last thank you *actually* goes to you! Thanks for being the most badass role model a daughter could ask for, and so much more. I'd like to think this book would have found a way to exist in the world without my help, but thank you for letting me take over its story and weave together so many incredible voices. Also, thank you for always supporting my writing dreams—all my dreams, really. You've always encouraged me, and you will never truly be able to know how much that has meant to me, or how lucky I feel to have that kind of support system.

ABOUT THE AUTHORS

DEAN HALL

Dean is a Licensed Clinical Marriage and Family Therapist and coach with over thirty years and more than 50,000 face-to-face hours of experience. He is an author, public speaker, and two-time cancer survivor. He is the first person to have swum both the Willamette River in Oregon, U.S.A. and the River Shannon in Ireland. He is working on his next river adventure and currently resides in Portland, Oregon, with his wife, Bobbi.

BRE HALL

Bre is a novelist who dabbles in nonfiction. She holds two degrees in creative writing: a BA from Pacific University and an MFA from American College Dublin. Her short fiction has appeared in various online journals and her debut adult novel, *Leave it Buried,* is set to be published in the spring of 2023. Having been raised in the flatlands of Kansas, Bre, a soul tied to the ocean, feels lucky nowadays to call the Oregon Coast home.

Made in the USA
Monee, IL
12 April 2023

31707062R00118